IN OUR OWN HOUSE

SOCIAL
PERSPECTIVES
ON
CANADIAN
LITERATURE

Edited by

PAUL CAPPON

McClelland and Stewart

McClelland and Stewart Limited
The Canadian Publishers
25 Hollinger Road, Toronto

Printed and bound in Canada

Canadian Cataloguing in Publication Data

Main entry under title:

In our own house

Bibliography: p.
ISBN 0-7710-1899-1

1. Canadian literature (English)–History and
criticism–Addresses, essays, lectures.*
2. Literature and society–Addresses, essays,
lectures. I. Cappon, Paul.

PS8077.15 C810'.9 C78-001126-0
PR9185.2.I5

Contents

PREFACE

There has occurred in the last decade a strong revival of interest in Canadian literature. Although this interest is unevenly felt in the various regions, and despite the gigantic problems faced by Canadian publishing houses, Canadian literature stubbornly refuses to play the role assigned to "colonial cultures." Against all odds, and certainly against the expectations given by massive American dominance in the economic, political and cultural domains, our literature appears to be doing much better than merely surviving. George Woodcock claims: "(The review) *Canadian Literature* merely celebrated the fact that Canadian writing had come of age; the emergence of a Canadian tradition of criticism confirmed the fact."[1]

The fact that Canadian literature presently refuses to "roll over and play dead" does not mean that its survival may never be threatened, together with Canadian cultural traditions generally. There exist at least two related ways by which we may ensure a continuous development of Canadian culture and of Canadian literature specifically: the first is to alter the economic conditions which restrain it, and the second is to understand the social meanings of Canadian literature, so that we may put this understanding to work. It is the development of such an understanding, with its implication for changes at basic economic and social levels, that must be the aim of a coherent sociology of Canadian literature.

The sociology of literature as a sub-discipline may at first appear suspect to the North American observer. When we consider that the dominant empiricist tradition in American sociology turned only recently to the arts as a suitable field of enquiry (because the arts appeared to be a less fruitful source of sociological "facts"), the further specialization of the sociology of Canadian literature seems preposterous. The purpose of this book, however, is not the creation of a sub-sub-field; nor is it, in accordance with the worst and most consistent orientations of American-dominated Canadian sociology, the tardy application to Canada of methods and subjects which have already been accepted as legitimate areas of sociological research in the U.S. On the contrary, its general purpose is to affirm the close relationship between the arts on the one hand and social and economic structures on the other, arts representing not simply a source of data on Canadian society, but also an important vehicle for social change. In other words, we must study literature not only to accumulate "facts" but to illuminate fundamental aspects of social structure as well as the necessity for change. The study proposed is specifically the sociology of Canadian literature, not merely because there is an expansion of literary activity in Canada but because the approaches must be responsive to the peculiar problems of Canadian literature.

It is therefore neither in a spirit of "cultural nationalism" nor of knowledge for its own size that this book is presented; the book is a response to the necessity for Canadians to appropriate the components of their culture, not only for individual aesthetic uses but also for the understanding of the function of artistic criticism as an agent of social change.

Although this book is the first in English Canada which attempts specifically to analyze literary activity from a social perspective, it is preceded by a number of writings which deal to some extent with the social meanings of Canadian literature. The work of Northrop Frye and other literary critics represented a meagre beginning; but the vulgarization and extension of some of their concepts contained in Margaret Atwood's *Survival* involved a real attempt at developing some understanding of the broad social implications of Canadian literature. More germane to this development have been numerous articles on Canadian literature in the better periodicals, especially *This Magazine*; and the work of George Woodcock and Miriam Waddington. In the pictorial arts, Barry Lord's *The History of Painting in Canada: Toward a People's Art* places Canadian painting squarely in the social domain for the first time. Instead of presenting our painting as a patchwork of schools and styles, Lord develops an historical approach based upon the social meaning of the work of art, relating this clearly to the artist's role in society and class position. The aesthetic values of works of art are demystified by being placed clearly in their social connexions. Lord gives ordinary people the tools by which they can judge art and appropriate it for collective social uses. The present book has a similar object with respect to literature.

As the first book of its kind the volume has obvious limitations: it is meant only as a beginning of a sociology of literature specific to Canada. There is no rigorous attempt to make analytical distinctions amongst the various literary forms as they relate to Canadian society. And the reference is only to English Canadian literature. Québécois literature, while faced with some of the same problems, must really be studied as a separate entity.

P.C.

Note to Preface

1. G. Woodcock, *Odysseus Ever Returning: Essays on Canadian Writers and Writing* (Toronto: McClelland and Stewart, 1970), p. 143.

GENERAL INTRODUCTION PART A: LITERATURE AND SOCIETY

PAUL CAPPON

The background to this book not only derives from works written about the arts in Canada, but its approach is founded on a general theoretical position – historical materialism. While this position does suggest points of departure for a sociology of Canadian literature, the peculiarities of the Canadian context determine certain emphases on specific problems. This introductory essay therefore consists of two parts. The first is an examination of the principal theoretical positions taken in sociology generally, and their applications to literature in particular. The second elucidates some critical problems in the development of an historical materialist analysis of Canadian literature.

Two Opposing Positions

When we consider the social origins and meanings of works of art and literature, the procedures which we employ will of course determine our final judgements about them. There exists *no one objective method* which will yield infallibly the social content and import of a single work, or groups of work. This is not surprising. After all, when one seeks the opinion of several different persons about one work, the opinions expressed are almost certain to diverge. Such a minor survey, then, should tell us as much about the ideas of the persons surveyed concerning art and its functions as it would about the works themselves.

Similarly, the approach adopted in the exmination of art and literature from a social, as opposed to strictly esthetic perspective, will reveal the theoretical and even the general political positions of the person conducting the study. Furthermore, since one's judgements regarding the social nature of an art work affect esthetic judgment or taste, the kind of position adopted by those who write about art and literature could also have a profound impact upon the social and political ideas of the public. An obvious example is the dominance in North American society of novels by writers like Norman Mailer or Leonard Cohen which, in their "modernism," emphasize the alienation of the individual to the point of neurosis. That powerful tastemakers (such as publishers, critics and granters of money) have chosen to make them popular, instead of writers who emphasize the potential for change collectively generated, reveal their own feeling of powerlessness, as well as resistance to radical social change. Would such a mood of desperate apathy so pervade North American society today if this attitude were not disseminated by a majority of writing and art, from the relatively high level of a Mailer or a Cohen to the relatively low level of a TV soap opera or "crime drama?" Would not the possibilities for bringing about social change through social movements be much improved if we had more evidence, through the medium of art, that alienation can be overcome when collective power for change is exercised?

Apologists for the pervasive individualist modernism argue that this artistic form does portray the world as it really is. The individual is alienated, isolated, powerless. A tiny minority does (or should, depending on different views) inevitably exercise power.[1] The only solutions are limited and individual, a choice among evils, involving withdrawal, neurosis or individual heroism.

Proponents of a more activist and collectivist stance in literature as in the real world will argue the opposite view. They will claim that profound social change is part of the historical process. As historical and economic elements necessary for changes appear, it is within the power of people acting collectively to produce those changes. Art and literature then should realistically reflect contemporary historical conditions, and the changes that may occur through human effort.

Clearly, trends and tastes in art and literature are founded on much more than individual whims and fancies. They are based on the currency given to a particular world view, which when translated into social science, becomes a theoretical and political position. We see from the above examples that the criticism of literature, as well as its study from a social perspective, takes as point of departure some already given notion of what constitutes the real world which is to be shown in literature. The two examples concerning the individual and collectivist positions may be taken as models describing the dominant and opposing critical positions in this essay. There exist variations on these models, but these two models will allow us to see how differing interpretations may be placed on the value and function of literature.

Our two models could provide two distinct "sociologies" of literature. In this book, we select one general position as superior to the other in the Canadian context. However, it is necessary to understand the opposing view because, as part of the dominant ideology of North American society, it forms the conditions under which literature and literary criticism are produced in this country. It helps to fashion people's tastes and to establish trends which must influence all artistic production and distribution. We therefore begin with the exposition of the dominant model, which we term "liberal sociology," and show its application to literature. Subsequently, we describe the historical materialist model which is employed in this book, and begin to use it in the discussion of problems of a specific sociology of Canadian literature.

Liberal Sociology

Of the two principal models or approaches used in the sociological study of literature, "liberal sociology" dominates in North America, as it dominates the whole field of American social science. Liberalism as the pervading mode of social scientific thought in North America has its roots firmly in the intellectual tradition of empiro-positivism. This tradition assumes that reality is empirical, that reality is a question of establishing all the observable facts which describe it. The origins of this tradition may be traced back to the famous philosophers and scientists of the Renaissance and of the Enlightenment. Inspired by a virulent anti-clericalism, and a hatred of the Middle Ages and of all the superstition, injustice and oppression which accompanied it, these philosophers would make Reason king. The Church, as religious and ideological bulwark of the feudal system, placed no high value on secular knowledge. Indeed, as is popularly known by the story of the persecution of Galileo by the Church as late as the seventeenth century, its authorities attempted to maintain a monopoly on knowledge, operating a system of strict censorship through control over its dissemination. Secular knowledge accumulated by the practice of science had value only insofar as it could have a religious function. Feudal society had no sense of plurality in human pursuits; it was an "organic" society in which all human endeavour was seen to be subsumed by religious goals. In such an atmosphere, it was impossible for any individual to legitmate the pursuit of knowledge for its own sake.

It is important to recognize that the decline of Church monopoly on knowledge at the close of the Middle Ages, and the beginnings of the acquisition of knowledge by empirical methods (observation), takes place at the time of the rise of capitalism, and positivism becomes the dominant mode of thought concurrent with the bourgeois revolutions of the seventeenth and eighteenth centuries. Empiro-positivism is thus historically tied to bourgeois society itself. The link between this mode of thought and the existence of bourgeois society lies in the fact that only through the rise of capitalism do the members of the bourgeoisie, who now own the means of production, become the dominant class. The ascendancy of capitalism and the bourgeoisie destroys not only the feudal economic system, but also the social, ideological and political structures of feudalism. The Church, as a primary element in the political and ideological structure, is no longer the only legitimate source of values, norms and ideas. The new values replacing honour, loyalty, obedience, and collectivism are the bourgeois values – equality, competition, individualism.

Under this new bourgeois ideology, knowledge becomes a key tool in the middle-class struggle to defeat the last vestiges of the feudal system. It is through the use of scientific and technological advance that nascent capitalism is able to raise the level of productive forces of the society, and to generate the profits which ensure its total victory against the old land-owning and clerical ruling class under feudalism. The pursuit of knowledge thus acquires a secular aim. Moreover, the growing individualism allowed by the new system permits individual scientists to legitimate whatever work they may undertake, since they are no longer obliged to submit all endeavour to the higher aims of ecclesiastical authority.

The result was a tremendous surge in scientific methods using induction and an attempt to blot out the scholastic, obscurantist and metaphysical reasoning of the feudal era by the demand for empirical proof through observation. Francis Bacon in the early seventeenth century was among the first to develop this empiro-positivism as a method. "Whereas the Aristotelian Schoolmen argued from established major premises (taken from past authority and the revelations of religion), Bacon wanted to shift and reverse the perspective" (Warhaft [ed.] p. 10).

> There are and can be only two ways of searching into and discovering truth. The one flies from the senses and particulars to the most general axioms, and from these principles, the truth of which it takes for settled and immovable, proceeds to judgment and to the discovery of middle axioms. And this way is now in fashion. The other derives axioms from the senses and particulars, rising by a gradual and unbroken ascent, so that it arrives at the most general axioms last of all. This is the true way, but as yet untried. (Bacon in Warhaft's selection of Bacon's works, p. 10)

This is an excellent early statement of positivism, the currently widely accepted "true way."

In *New Atlantis* Bacon demonstrates the uses of his method for scientists and industrialists. The method, based as it was on observable "facts," not only appealed to the hard-headed realism of the early bourgeois, but it also resulted in the rapid technical advances which increased production and profit. Small wonder that this positivist approach has been associated with bourgeois society ever since.

Bacon's empiricism became the accepted model as bourgeois society developed, passed on by Descartes, Newtonian physics and the natural sciences to the social sciences which developed after the completion of bourgeois hegemony at the beginning of the nineteenth century. Thus we find that all social science, from the sociology of its "founder," Auguste Comte, through history became dominated by the positivist tradition. The famous German historian Leopold von Ranke, spoke for all empiricists in remarking that the task of the historian was simply "to show how it really was." E. H. Carr, whose 1961 book *What is History*?, played an important role in debunking positivism, makes equally valid statements for sociology:

> First ascertain the fact, said the Positivists, then draw your conclusions from them. In Great Britain, this view of history fitted perfectly with the empiricist tradition which was the dominant strain of British philosophy from Locke to Bertrand Russell. The empirical theory of knowledge pre-supposes a complete separation between subject and object. Facts, like sense impressions, impinge on the observer from outside, and are independent of his consciousness. The process of reception is passive: having received the data, he then acts on them.... This is what may be called the common-sense view of history. History consists of a corpus of ascertained facts. The facts are available to the historian in documents, inscriptions and so on, like fish on the fishmonger's slab. The historian takes them home, and cooks and serves them in whatever style appeals to him. (E. H. Carr: p. 9)

It is true for the sociologist as for the historian that the establishment of something as a fact rests essentially on a personal and subjective decision. The social scientist as well as the historian arbitrarily selects and arranges his "facts."

> It used to be said that facts speak for themselves. This is, of course, untrue. The facts speak only when the historian calls

> on them: it is he who decided to which facts to give the floor, and in what order or context. It was, I think, one of Pirandello's characters who said that a fact is like a sack – it won't stand up till you've put something in it. The belief in a hard core of historical facts existing objectively and independently of the interpretation of the historian is a preposterous fallacy, but one which is very hard to eradicate. (E. H. Carr: p. 11)

The original positivist programme of sociologists, then, was aimed at "the collection of facts, to be followed by the framing of general laws comparable to those of Newtonian physics" (Gareth Jones: p. 97). "On the methodological level, they were 'scientistic," stressing the objective external character of social reality and the naturalism of social study" (Martin Shaw: p. 35). It is important to note that only when the belief in progress inherent in liberalism is threatened does empiro-positivism come into serious doubt.

> In the period of "classical sociology," at the end of the last century and the beginning of this – the period of the crisis of classical imperialism – the belief in social progress collapsed, and the methodological certainties of positivism were enveloped in doubt. In the work of Max Weber, for example, a pessimistic perspective of global bureaucratization replaces evolutionary optimism. And in his methodology, the surviving elements of positive social science are surrounded by cultural relativism and subjectivism. This . . . was a typical movement. It was an expression of the real crisis of traditional conservatism and liberalism in the fact of the juggurnaut of imperialism and the direct challenge of social revolution. Another classical sociologist, Wilfred Pareto, could only find a way out by supporting the first steps in Mussolini's development of the fascist state. (Martin Shaw: p. 35-36)

Thus we see that the smooth development of capitalist society, the belief in progress, and liberalism are all bound up with the empiro-positivist method. This perception allows us to understand why this liberal approach should always find its firmest footing in the Western countries in the forefront of capitalist development, first in Britain, then in the United States. Liberal sociology, like liberal economics, with all its assumptions about the competition and individualism inherent in human nature, has completely dominated the American academic tradition; and from it has passed to Canada by way of the colonial connexion as manifested at the level of ideology and education.

In American "mainstream" sociology, the empiricist method has meant the *description* of what is most observable in society. Their hope is to discover the separate parts of reality, assuming that these separate parts accumulated will reveal the total reality. Such a descriptive study is like a snapshot of social phenomena. If the snapshots can be fitted together like a jigsaw puzzle, empiricists may fully understand social reality. This process makes two dubious assumptions about society. The first is that a description of the observable is indeed more true or "objective" than a non-descriptive, conceptual approach. This is the positivist element: "facts speak for themselves, once they are properly discovered." But this assumption is very like assuming that a snapshot contains more objectivity or truth than a painting. If this were so, landscape, portrait and other painters might long since have gone out of business.

The second assumption is that the partial analysis of empiricism, in accumulating selected information about social phenomena, can ever tell as anything significant about the whole. It presumes that the totality is composed of the separate parts added together. The historical materialist view of totality takes the opposite position. It asks the kind of question which D. H. Carr has posed: Does not the continual pursuit of "facts" which are selected by the social scientist according to the prior dictates of his own position lead to a misrepresentation of reality? If one concentrates on what is presently observable (snapshot) to the exclusion of the historical process which creates phenomena, is there any chance at all of explaining reality?

When, armed with this empiro-positivist view of reality based on observable "facts," traditional American sociology comes to study North American society, it seems a multiplicity of social groupings. There are corporations, governments, lobbies, trade unions, ladies auxiliaries, political parties, women's movements, armed forces, intellectuals, charities, men's clubs, artists, writers. It seems apparent that the society is a pluralist one in which no one small group can completely dominate. It is true that elites exist, but there are many kinds of elites, from the corporate through the trade union to the Hollywood. Among these elites is stiff competition for power and prestige. Additionally, the elites may be "circulating," with different ones achieving more or less power at different times. Finally, the composition of the elites changes over time, given a degree of access to them which is relatively high in comparison with previous or other societies.

From this view it is an easy step to the perception that this pluralist, liberal society is superior because of its balance, because no one group or authority is allowed so to upset the equilibrium that it acquires directive power. North American society would then be *structured* in such a way that its many facets may have as part of their *function* the maintenance of this equilibrium. This *structural-functionalist* perspective has become the dominant one within American positivist sociology. Alex Inkeles (1964) gives a typical description of the structural-functionalist perspective when he states that it emphasizes the function of institutions in co-ordinating society. This view of society is a static one: it attempts to show how structures or institutions keep society in operation. By analyzing the structures and functions of all the institutions of a society and studying how they are co-ordinated and integrated, we can outline the conditions of social life, and trace the process by which society arranges to meet its needs.

The equilibrium model of Talcott Parsons (1953) is a variation on structural-functionalism. The equilibrium theory, like the corresponding one in liberal economics, maintains that society has a system of automatic adjustments to redress the balance when it is upset by internal or external forces. The following example may serve to illustrate how this view is connected with the dominant ideology of middle-class society: the model would assume that an "extremist" reaction, like the election of an Allende in Chile or the strength of Communist parties in many countries, is an expression of *dysfunction* of societal, political or economic institutions, like corruption or economic crisis. Once the dysfunction is corrected, the function served by the popular radical expression is terminated, and one would expect them normally to return to more moderate behaviour.

A variation on the equilibrium model itself is the conflict model, of which Lewis Coser (1956) has been a principal exponent. This perspective is also interested in the maintenance of the status quo, but this time through conflict rather than through adjustment. The basic premise is dissension, not consensus, but the result is similar.

At the centre of all of these variations on the structural-functional model, based on empiro-positivist method, is the study of institutions. According to this perspective "a set of institutions constitutes a social system, of which the institutions may be thought of as sub-systems" (Inkeles; p. 68). Presumably, once the various types of institutions have been described (their structure) and their function analyzed, we would arrive at some understanding of society. Thus for Inkeles, institutions "constitute the building blocks of society" (Inkeles: p. 67). Each type of institution has a *function* in the maintenance of social life, and the shaping of society.

Because the empiricist method is essentially a static one, having as its goal the description of what appear to the liberal sociologist to be social facts, the various institutions are studied largely in isolation (partial analysis). While it is assumed that there will be some overlap among them, it is not considered that one institution can dominate a pluralist society like North America; and even less that the observable institutions might themselves be products of more fundamental social forces. Thus for Inkeles, there exist four main types of institutions:

> First there are the *political institutions* concerned with the exercise of power and which have a monopoly on the legitimate use of force.... Second, there are the economic institutions, concerned with the production and distribution of goods and services. *Expressive-integrative* institutions, including those dealing with the arts, drama and recreation, represent a third set.... *Kinship institutions*, the fourth main category, are principally focussed around the problem of regulating sex and providing a stable framework for the rearing of the young. (Inkeles: p. 68)

We may note that each of Inkeles' institutional types or *structures* has a distinct function, that none controls the others, and that each can be studied as a separate social "building block" in an empirical way, in order to learn some truth about the social system. We will be contrasting this with the historical materialist position, which is that economic forces dominate society and are instrumental in shaping a dominant social class which in turn forms the institutions which are necessary to its rule; and that empirical description of the above institutions will therefore yield only a false image of social reality.

For historical materialist analysis, economic evolution determines the development of social class contradictions, and this historic class struggle is at the centre of its attention. All subjects of social scientific thought, including literature, will take this as a point of departure. For the empiricist structural-functionalist also, social class is as critical a problem as institutions, for the whole pattern of society will reflect class structure. It is therefore important to describe the contrasting perspectives of liberal sociology and of historical materialism on social class, not only because this will point out crucial differences in their methods, but also because these differences will colour the analysis which will be made up of a social phenomenon like the production of literature.

In keeping with its empiricism, structural-functionalists use a descriptive theory called *social stratification*. "Social stratum" is the central term. It enables them by the application of such variables as income, social prestige, occupational prestige, consciousness of one's own position in society etc., to place people into a hierarchy of socio-economic groupings. Hence the terms upper-class, middle-class etc. This description of hierarchy enables us to place a given person into a given socio-economic bracket;[2] and so doing, helps us to correlate the situation of individuals making up that bracket with its collective behaviour, especially its political behaviour, including voting patterns. But the use of the study of social strata for the study of the dynamics of society and its propensity for fundamental change is very limited; social stratum includes not only income variables and socio-occupational prestige, but even the feelings which a person has about the stratum to which he belongs. Thus, almost all Canadians think that they belong to the middle stratum of society, the "middle class." Consider the contrast of such a theory with the Marxist theory of classes. In the first instance, class contradictions are played down or denied. We would not be considering conflict between capitalists and workers, the first class making a profit from its capital and the second having only its labour to sell; rather we have a muddled social hierarchy which obscures class lines. Note that, depending on the detail of the scale use, the descriptive model could define any number of "classes." There could be upper, middle and lower. A more refined version would yield strata ad nauseum!

In practice, everyone but the highest and the lowest are encouraged to think of themselves as part of the middle class, even if some are richer than others. This notion of middle class is bolstered by ideological constructs like the idea of equality before the law, the ability to lobby and to join clubs, the equal power of the universal ballot. The difference between richer and poorer is therefore not viewed as the result of class contradictions and exploitation but simply in a descriptive way. Thus, the carpenter making $12,000 and the businessman making $35,000 are different only insofar as the former belongs to a lower socio-economic stratum, not in the fact that one must sell his labour to the businessman who makes a profit on this capital investment.

In the liberal theory of social stratification, one of the important areas of study would be social mobility – the facility with which individuals can move from one stratum to another. If elites are said to be competitive, then the rate of vertical mobility must be a key variable in determining that our societies are not ruled by a power elite,[3] but rather by a series of independent elites, as Inkeles would have us believe. Liberals will claim that no matter how high the rate of social mobility, social stratification is justified by its own inevitability. This is, of course, the ideological basis for the whole theory: "There is good reason to assume that ranking people is inherent in man, and that no society will ever be without it" (Inkeles: p. 83).

What is the relationship between the liberal structuralist-functionalism, based on empiro-positivism and the theoretical, ideological and political positions on which it is actually based? We have seen that the premises of structural-functionalist thought are the successful functioning of institutions, the necessity in any society of social stratification (inequality), and the social mobility which allows people to pass from one stratum to another – thereby creating competition among elites for power. This political competition is analagous to economic competition in capitalist entrepreneurship; these two form the basis for liberal political thought. There are therefore two essential ideological and political notions in this system: first, that social and occupational mobility is highly possible and desirable, and second, that even given unequal distribution of economic resources, all strata of society, including the "lower middle-class," be able to exercise some political power through interest-group lobbying (unions) and through the vote. This is the divorce of the political and social man which Marx states is a mystification of reality.

Institutions play a key role in the ordering of social strata through the division of labour. More competent people may be entrusted with a job requiring greater skill – which is rewarded by higher prestige and remuneration. On the political level, the highest institutional regulator of activity (*structure*) is the State. It *functions*, through democratic voting procedures as the structure within which elites compete and circulate, subject to the disapproval of the citizens. It must also arbitrate between the different factions and parts of the social strata, ensuring the maintenance of economic and political competition.

In political terms, the highest level that may be reached by liberal, pluralist society is political democracy and a State which performs the function of a neutral arbitrator among the plethora of interests and groups. Hence, a society must become politically more democratic while developing increased socio-economic mobility. This vertical social mobility is somehow connected with a wider sharing of wealth; and it is the hope of liberals like Inkeles that this will lead, in an open-class system, to political democracy.

In this democracy or pluralist society, a liberal political scientist like Kornhauser (1959) would argue that as many constraints on the individual are removed as is consistent with the freedom of others (Kornhauser p. 23). This notion of freedom is related to the competitiveness in society due to social mobility between strata and the circulation of elites. Freedom is essentially *individual*. In Kornhauser's pluralist society elites are competitive and must therefore be accessible to the mass of the people. The mass of the population, on the other hand, must not be mobilized by the elite for political purposes, as it can in mass society (like "totalitarian" Communism), because people have multiple commitments to diverse and autonomous groups – that multiplicity of groups we earlier stated to be the most observable social phenomenon for the empiricist. These groups, as well as larger institutions in society, carry out the function of splitting people into different roles, so that the "democratic system" remains unendangered. Political activity outside these existing institutions (especially the vote) can lead to serious *dysfunctions* and is therefore dangerous to stable democracy (Kornhauser: p. 46).

The key to political democracy in the liberal system is therefore the *institutionalization* of political and social processes. Any dissatisfaction with inequalities is neutralized when channelled through institutional activity. It is thus explicit in Kornhauser and implicit in the whole of liberal functionalist thought (and is reflected in the three major Canadian political parties) that institutions are functional in the sense of regulating conflict, therefore "good"; while extra-institutional activity is dysfunctional, and is the result of some social disequilibrium. Nothing better illustrates this structural-functionalist view, in opposition to a Marxist or non-liberal view, than Kornhauser's appraisal of American unions like the AFL-CIO. These are necessary for the institutionalization and neutralization of any serious conflict between classes (Kornhauser p. 96-97).

Liberal Sociology and Literature

We have attempted to show, in the foregoing passage, that liberal sociology, as one of the two basic perspectives that can be taken on the social scientific study of literature and art, is based on a series of interconnected positions. First and foremost, it is *premised* on the ideological and political positions of liberalism. Liberalism itself may be said to be the prevailing mode of thought of bourgeois society, supportive of the precepts of capitalist society and running its career parallel to that of capitalism. Empiro-positivism, as the social scientific *method* usually adopted under liberal sociology, also has its roots firmly in the development and in the career of thought in middle-class society, and ends up supporting liberalism's ideological premises. Structural-functionalism is the combination of liberal ideological premises and the empiricist method in the tackling of a particular social problem, like social stratification.

The whole liberal system of thought is so profoundly influential that its truth is widely taken for granted in middle-class society. It shapes the dominant ideology in North America, thereby aiding social control. So implicit is it in most writings touching social issues that most authors, even sociologists, are unaware of their own ideological presuppositions, and do not state them as initial positions. This is why we must be very careful, in showing the method of individual liberal sociologists, to link them with the whole complex of liberal thought with all its implications.

When we come to consider the liberal position with respect to the study of literature, we see that the foremost of these implications is the formation of values which would also colour the author's view of literature. Most important among these values are individualism, relativism, knowledge for its own sake. Individualism is implicit in the whole liberal theory of social stratification with its emphasis on the mapping out of the position of the *individual*, and on *individual* social mobility; as contrasted with the importance of collectivities like classes in Marxist theory. Relativism is explicit in the notion that there exists a human nature which is responsible for the inevitable existence of class and inequality. Implicit then is the idea that the middle-class notion of individual "freedom" within a "political democracy" is the best possible solution relative to all others, and that effort must be made to preserve the general status quo in places, like North America, which have already achieved it. Individualism combines with relativism, as we have seen with Kornhauser, to produce suspicion and hostility towards fundamental social change collectively generated; and this hostility, grounded in politics and ideology, is sometimes masqueraded as the "pure science" of empiricism. Inkeles again provides us with a typical example.

> The issue comes down to that of the legitimacy of pure science. Those who urge an engaged, critical practical problem-centred sociology certainly have a right to their preference.... Where the activist goes wrong is in questioning the legitimacy of any other kind of social science, especially the kind which aspires to meet the conditions of pure science. (Inkeles: p. 104)

This apparent tolerance of other views, another trade-mark of liberalism, is easy enough when those who dominate the institutions of dissemination of education and ideology are of this persuasion. We see hear the clear advantage to the status quo of not doing "engaged, critical, practical, problem-centred" research, but of doing strictly empirical research instead. Empirical approaches generate "facts" or "knowledge" for its own sake. What began during the Renaissance and the Enlightenment as a method which opposed sicence to Church monopoly (in order to end feudalism) ends up under advanced capitalism as a system which opposes research specifically directed at social change. It posits, in relativistic fashion, that any field or problem, taken from any political position, is equally valid, as long as the analyst is "objective." Inkeles beautifully sums up this mixture of individualism, relativism and knowledge for its own sake (even, as historical materialists claim, it ends up mystifying, not clarifying reality).

> For many sociologists the prime consideration is the advancement of knowledge.... the critical issue is whether the conduct of the research follow the rules set down by scientific procedure.... In a civilized world a man should be free to choose the position he finds congenial. As a politically active person you may criticize him for his inactivity. But as a sociologist your evaluation of him should rest on the quality and adequacy of his research. The universal standard of judgment for that purpose is the degree to which he advances knowledge of man and society.... If the activists had their way, we might ultimately be led to "directed" research in which some public authority would choose the problems on which social scientists must work. Anyone with even the

faintest knowledge of totalitarian countries like Soviet Russia or Nazi Germany knows this means the initial perversion and ultimately the complete destruction of all social science. (Inkeles: p. 103–104)

The foregoing summary gives us a clear picture of the way liberal sociology would undertake the study of literature, and even of the general attitude of liberals towards art. In the first instance, as empiricists they would be interested primarily in art as a document which provides knowledge about a society, which provides another way of helping to describe it. Because they view the expressive-integrative institutions of a society as functional, they would compare art forms cross-culturally in order to compare societies. As functionalists, they would assume that, if an art form or practice exists, and certainly if it dominates, it is performing some kind of integrative social function. Compare this with the historical materialist view that educational and artistic institutions are directed by a dominant class and will largely reflect its values (those of capitalist society); and that the study of literature must include the analysis of this control and of the art forms which it typically produces. What will therefore be critical for the historical materialist is not only art as a document but the conditions of its production and distribution under the capitalist market system. The liberal perspective will also be interested in the artist and the writer, but their interest will take the ethnographic form of study of art as a "lifestyle" different from other kinds. The historical materialist, on the other hand, will want to study artists and writers in order to discern the specific ways in which the conditions of production and distribution determine the content and style of their work.

In the second instance, liberals' attitudes towards art and literature will parallel their views about social science. Individualism is exemplified by the position that the pessimistic modern novels of alienation and individualized response to social problems on the purely psychological level is showing reality as it is. The liberal theories of social mobility and political democracy imply that "freedom" is essentially individual. What is therefore more appropriate than that different individuals should seek it in various ways, depending on their psychological make-up; and that this should be reflected in the popularity of individualistic literature? Compare this again with the historical materialist view which will argue that it is essentially the organization of production and distribution under the capitalist market system which determines the popularity of works which reflect bourgeois values and interests.

Both individualism and relativism are present in the liberal position that artistic works should be judged on their esthetic value, independent of their social content. For a historical materialist, the two are interconnected. For a liberal, trying to make the relative best in a bad situation of human nature tainted with insurmountable flaws, art is the accomplishment of a single individual, even if it does no more than to feed off a society. Kenneth Clark states in concluding *Civilization*: "Above all, I believe in the God-given genius of certain individuals, and I value a society which makes their existence possible" (p. 347).

The empiro-positivist doctrine of "knowledge" for its own sake is parallelled by liberals' essential belief in "art for art's sake." This is not the place to trace the parallel development of this notion and of capitalism itself,[4] but it suffices to say that this is analogous with the growth of empiricism in social science. "Art for art's sake" is an inevitable consequence of liberal relativism. If one cannot adjudge art and literature on social grounds, but only on esthetic values (assuming their independence), then no particular form or work of art can be advanced as having more value than another. Naturally enough in middle-class society, it becomes a question of indivdual taste. The production of a work of literature can no more be accepted or condemned on social grounds than the choice between two brands of detergent. For the historical materialist, it is precisely the fact that it is the same economic forces and dominant class which control the production of both art and detergent which make their study crucial; because the consumer's "choice" in both cases is determined beforehand by the organization of production and distribution. In both cases, the "freedom of choice" is equally illusory. Someone largely controls taste in literature as in after-shave lotion.

Liberal Sociology Applied to Literature

Before turning to the definition of the historical materialist position and its uses in the study of literature, it is useful to show some applications of the liberal approach. The French nineteenth-century philosopher Taine was the first to apply Auguste Comte's positivist sociology to literature. As an empiricist he "frequently uses literature as a document, and throughout his writings there runs a strong reductionist element. He has no conception of the literary text as the focal point of research." (Laurenson and Swingewood: p. 39.) For Taine the novel is no more than "an accumulation of data which, through the operation of scientific laws would fall into inevitable patterns."[5] As Swingewood declares:

> Clearly any literary sociology which bases itself on such clear-cut positivism as this – literature as a source of information or documentation – can and must be prepared to study all kinds of literature, good, bad and indifferent, since the problem is simply one of objective material causation and reflection. But like many sociologists Taine is loath to draw this conclusion." "Literary works," he argues, "furnish documents because they are monuments." (Swingewood, p. 32)

Taine's dilemma is the contradiction between literature purely as a document and his desire to allow some autonomy of the creative spirit. His solution, so common in empiro-positivism, is to smuggle in an idealist construct to give some satisfying significance to the labour of documentation, to allow him to say that some works are better documents than others. The positivist pretensions to sociology as a science do not allow him to admit that there is already a "bias" in the work of studying only "monumental" literature. Occasionally, these scientistic pretentions are betrayed by frank statements of political views which give away the liberal premises. Thus, although Kenneth Clark[6] talks of different competing elites, he also admits to the belief that art necessarily created for ruling elites is proper. He says that there "exists an elite, not necessarily in a political sense, but in a spiritual and intellectual sense ... it may be drawn from any class of society" (Clark: p. 635).

But he goes on to state: "All art is waste in a material sense; and the idea that things should be made more precious looking in accordance with the status of the user seems to me entirely fitting. I would go further and say that ornament is inseparable from hierarchy. It is not only the result but the cause of status ... (Art is) created by a minority: yes, but accepted by the majority unquestioningly, eagerly and with a sense of participation" (Clark: p. 238). Clark, beginning from positivistic premises, has ended up with either "art for art's sake"; or an idealism which claims that, although art is created for a minority, that's all right because the majority accepts willingly this state of affairs.

It would not be unfair to say that the standard application of empiro-positivism to the arts has revealed itself to make many idealistic assumptions which support the class system. This critique of positivism in literature is best described by Christopher Caudwell as early as the 1930's.

> Positivism is always dishonest and from the very start smuggles in another reality (usually the mind) into the system in order to organize it and provide some standard of validity.[7] This reality will be concealed under some name such as "convenience" or "probability". Positivism is thus in fact generally shamefaced idealism or occasionally (in the form of agnosticism) shamefaced materialism.
>
> Positivism therefore appears in aesthetics as the pure act of enjoyment of the art work, as "art for art's sake". Of course this would give absolutely no standard of discrimination between art works of between enjoyments of art works, and therefore, in fact all aesthetic positivists smuggle in some organizing principle, generally emotionist (integration of the personality or reality of the emotion) but occasionally formal (rhythm or form). (Caudwell: p. 17)

As the empiricist method developed and structural-functionalism became the dominant American tradition, its application to the arts did not grow as quickly. This is simply because structural-functionalists like Parsons considered insitutions of the "expressive" type to be much less important to keep society well-oiled. "The sociology of literature is thus a fairly late arrival, for although there are today well-developed sociologies of religion, education, politics, social change, and even in so imprecise an area as ideology, there is virtually no established corpus of knowledge called the sociology of literature" (Laurenson and Swingewood: p. 13).

The only importance which Parsonian structural-functionalists could see in the social impact of the arts was naturally a functionalist, "balancing" one: "A society which makes the institutionalization of instrument roles very widespread must have, if it is to continue more or less stable, some compensatory mechanisms for the gratification of need-dispositions for immediate gratification" (Parsons and Shils: p. 425-426). Thus for example, highly charged emotional outlets like "romantic love, commercialized entertainment, drinking, and the literature and films of violence" may in fact be necessary in order to maintain social equilibrium, given "the one-sidedness of instrumental roles." Anything will do if it keeps the people "stable" – atomized, passive, quietly unresisting. This is the basis we have had for "mainstream" Canadian sociology!

Later structural-functionalists have attempted to show themselves less obviously oriented towards pacification of the people through artistic expression, and have tried to present arts as also a medium for social change. But it is always a controlled medium, an institution. We have seen that institutionalization of conflict and non-conformism in fact favours the status quo because it channels resistance into controlled and defined modes; and because institutions are themselves controlled by the dominant class. It is therefore clear that this new position, although placing more emphasis on expressive-integrative institutions than the Parsonian model, only allows the very limited social change which can do no fundamental harm to "democratic," "pluralist" society as it now operates.

> Art as an institution may be regarded as a minority culture that functions both for stability and for change in our complex pluralistic society. It may contribute to stability, not only by balancing emotional against instrumental needs or by releasing tensions, but also be providing congenial occupations and interests for "deviant" personalities. Those persons whose native tendencies and socialization are directed

> toward contemplation, for example, toward values of 'being' instead of 'doing', may find in art a mode of creativity expressive of their personality; others may find in related areas the means for fostering the values of art in society. Institutionalization of art activities thus becomes not only a stablizing element in society but also an enrichment of its 'value' resources. (Milton C. Albrecht: p. 14)

This is perhaps the most modern statement of liberal sociology's approach to the arts, containing most of the elements of the liberal system of thought. It atomizes individuals, emphasizing varying "needs" and "tendencies." Tolerance should be shown towards those who "deviate" in artistic directions. This enables the sociologist (and politician) to treat modern art forms as simply a life-style and choice of certain individuals, not as a function of the existing economic, class and social structure as a whole. If people decide that they want to retire to the country and make bead necklaces, this is an individual choice generated by different needs, and one which should be accepted by others. Similarly, if others wish to make violent films, this individual choice should be explained as simply part of pluralist society and accepted as such. No explanation of the structural basis of this behaviour in the system of economic and artistic production or the class structure is offered. Institutionalization of the processes of artistic production is claimed to be a "stabilizing element in society": this is true. If artistic production can be carried on only under a given set of norms and rules as determined by the market system under capitalism, individuals are likely to remain isolated, subject as individual atoms to the rule of the powers of the market. Consequently, any art which is "deviant" in a socially significant sense, rather than an individual sense, is unlikely to prosper. This would naturally include that art which is directed toward radical social change. Not in accord with the material conditions of production and distribution of arts, it cannot gain wide acceptance until those conditions are altered.

The arts represent one of the last remaining social phenomena to which American mainstream, liberal sociology, as characterized by structural-functionalist notions, has still to be applied. Yet the whole liberal sociological framework is so permeated by the dominant ideology of North American liberalism that most writing on Canadian literature that takes any account of its social aspects incorporates individualism and elitism. Margaret Atwood's book *Survival* is the best known of these. It will be briefly discussed later in the essay, in comparison with the historical materialist approach.

The Historical Materialist Position

We have implied throughout the discussion of liberal sociology that the historical materialist method and its application to arts is in sharp contrast to the former. Contrary to the trend in all other areas, much of the work that has been done on the sociology of literature has been from a historical materialist perspective. This is because, unlike empiro-positivism, which conducts partial analysis of the observable, historical materialism begins with the idea that society represents a totality which is not the sum of its institutional parts. Social reality must be grasped as a unified whole. In this, it shares a similar conspectus with literature, which does not attempt simply to describe a piece of the world, but to express the writer's world view within a restricted framework.

Historical materialist sociology is not only concerned with institutions, socialization, and role-playing, but also with the processes of social change and the effects which these changes have on social structure. These social processes can be large-scale, like the transition from feudalism to capitalism, or internal: for example, the legitimation of authority and of ideology, of the ways in which conflict is regulated in different types of societies.

The concepts of *history* or change and *totality* are therefore the key elements in the historical materialist approach. It is insufficient to take a snapshot of what seems at present most observable: in order to understand contemporary society, we must understand the historical processes which produced it. In contrast to structural-functionalism, it is not assumed that contemporary institutions have a necessary balancing function; but rather that they play their role only within a specific historical context, and that they will be outmoded with transition to a further stage of social evolution. *Totality* implies that the historical process and its social product cannot be seen by dissection of isolated elements; that what is immediately apparent does not coincide with the essence of phenomena, as the positivists think. As the prominent literary sociologist Lucien Goldmann points out, the emphasis in historical materialism is on the structure of phenomena: "The chief problem of the social and historical sciences is that of working out the techniques by means of which it is possible to bring to light the principal elements the mixture of which constitute empirical reality" (Lucien Goldmann: p. 582). Thus the emphasis is on understanding what *underlies and creates* empirical reality: and this understanding will in fact give a completely different idea of what that reality really is. To revert to the analogy of the photograph and the painting, historical materialists would in no way view them as comparable: what is most important about the painting cannot be reproduced in a photograph – the unique conditions under which the painting is produced together with the state of mind of the artist as partially created by these conditions.

Totality implies an interconnectedness of all economic, social, and political phenomena which is ignored by the positivist method of looking at things in isolation, then piecing them together in the assumption that the accumulated parts constitute the whole. Interconnectedness means that the different economic, social and political institutions cannot but support each other. In any given historical situation, they must work for similar goals. This in turn implies that none of them can fundamentally change without the others, that is, without radical social change. Transition from feudalism to enterprise capitalism is considered to be an example of such radical change in which economic, social, political and ideological institutions and processes must have changed (not necessarily simultaneously) in the same direction. The transition from competitive to monopoly capitalism accounts for similar fundamental changes among all institutions. It is obvious how this theoretical position is related to a revolutionary view of capitalist society. It must posit that piecemeal change is not possible, and that the various structures of capitalist and other societies, being interrelated, must be all altered. Conversely, it is easy to see how liberalism, a revolutionary position (especially positivism) when the bourgeoisie was in revolt against feudal vestiges on the political and ideological levels, becomes oriented towards the status quo in bourgeois society. Its dealing with various phenomena in isolation implies, as we have seen with Albrecht's appraisal of art as an institution, that slow evolutionary change is possible within the confines of capitalist society generally by changing parts of society and institutions individually. Thus the two positions are opposing not simply in methodology but in the political and social outcomes towards which their premises orient them, and in the historical roles which they play in guiding popular thought in one direction or the opposing at crucial junctures.

The chief point of interconnectedness in historical materialist analysis of the total system is the economic, the *material conditions of production* of goods. This has often been misinterpreted to mean that economics inevitably dominates every phase of human activity. In fact, it means that the historical processes of change and the whole social structure, are not possible without a given system of material production. The historical development of societies is viewed as dependent on changes in the system of production or *economic substructure*. These changes in the economic substructure make possible, but at the same time require for their permanence, alterations in the social, political, and ideological *super-structures*. Feudalism, for example, was founded on a system of production which was essentially individual. Production was mainly in order to meet the needs of the producers' families, with little organized division of labour or socialized production. Accumulation of surplus was slow because of this "primitive" division of labour, and the surplus was disposed of according to no encompassing market system. Land was the principal means of production under this system, so that we find land-owning nobility as the ruling class which appropriated surplus production. The Church was dominant at the political and ideological levels. The political character of the times – no central national political authority but a universal political authority in the Church – was directly founded on a system of small-unit, isolated production. We have seen that the norms and values of the times, including honour, loyalty, obedience, religiosity, were directly necessary to support the social hierarchy or class structure, itself a result of the system of production. Under feudalism, although the economic substructure determines its essential character, the ideological and political as manifested in the Church appear to be the most important elements of the society, but only because these are crucial to the maintenance of the relations of production themselves.

Under the competitive capitalism of industrial society, production becomes socialized by the introduction of a complex division of labour with people working together and often under one roof. The production of labour is now appropriated by the capitalists. The ownership of the means of production in the hands of capitalists rather than landowners determines entirely new social relations of production under which capitalists become the new dominant class. Because production is now more socialized and rationalized, it is far more efficient and surpluses or profits are larger. This accumulating surplus requires the institution of extensive markets not only for the products themselves but also for the human labour which produces them. This economic substructure can therefore be seen as directly determinate of a political system of unified national states without which the necessary expansion of the market systems vital to capitalism cannot be achieved. Thus are political institutions like the State and parliamentary democracy entirely connected with the requirements of capitalism. The class system itself is viewed not as the descriptive hierarchy of the structural-functionalists but rather as the product of a dichotomy between owners and non-owners of the means of production. It is not primarily income together with other objective and subjective variables but the relations of production which determine class – and, usually, income and the other variables. Class is therefore viewed not as hierarchy of strata but rather as an opposition between owners and their agents and non-owners.

For structural-functionalists, the political system of parliamentary democracy elected through universal suffrage, combined with social mobility, tended to counterbalance the effects of income and status inequalities. But in the historical materialist perspective, the limited social mobility that exists does not alter the class structure or inequalities, it simply replaces some individuals and groups by others. Political and ideological superstructures, based as they are upon the specific relation of production and class system in capitalism, and inextricably connected with it, reinforce rather than diminish the effects of the system. Thus the State as the highest political institution is not seen as a neutral arbiter amongst classes and groups. Rather, in its structure and functioning via the parliamentary process, the civil service, and the dominance of institutional politics through political parties, it is viewed as the vehicle by which the bourgeoisie exercises its political power. (Ownership of the means of production and control over the market system are ways of exercising its economic power). In this totality of inter-related institutions based on the material conditions of production specific to capitalism, the ideological superstructure is perceived as also supportive of capitalism. The dominant ideology of capitalist society, like that of feudal, will be that of the dominant class. In the case of capitalism, equality, competition, and individualism are important values. The ruling class is viewed as controlling the institutions of Propagation of norms and values – educational institutions and media and art.

The transition from competitive to monopoly capitalism is also that of one totality to another, always with vestiges of the old system lagging on for some time after transition. Under monopoly capitalism, the form of ownership changes; the old entrepreneur is replaced by a dispersal of *legal* ownership to the relative many,[8] while *real* ownership of capital remains in the hands of a tiny ruling elite. A more complex division of labour necessary for even higher levels of productive activity creates a middle class whose function is partly managerial and partly that of collective worker. The transition to monopoly capitalism demands for its success reform in the political and ideological superstructures. Especially important on the political level would be increased intervention of the State to provide the physical (e.g. transportation) and human (e.g. management of labour market through manpower and immigration policies) infrastructure for the monopoly corporations. Without this measure of centralized State planning, which eventually becomes State capitalism, the more complex market and administration requirements of monopoly capitalism would not be able to function. Similarly on the ideological level, monopoly capitalism requires changes to value systems which will be more consistent with its functioning. In particular, educational and other institutions are called upon to invest people with more passive, less work-oriented values more consistent with the consumer society, also more in line with a monopoly capitalist society with its consistent underemployment of people and productive facilities.

North American society therefore appears to the historical materialist as an integrated whole whose various parts and institutions can be separately analyzed only insofar as they are seen as belonging to the totality of bourgeois society. This does not mean that no thought or action can occur which is not controlled by the dictates of capitalism, but that every social phenomenon must be seen in terms of it. When this is done, initiatives like the "hippie cult", which on the surface appear counter to capitalist society, in fact can be easily assimilated and even exploited by the dominant ideologies and classes. Similarly, art must be seen in its social connection not only in terms of the nature of its *form* (whether apparently revolutionary or conformist), but also in terms of its real historical role within the framework of monopoly capitalism. When looked at from this angle, much that appears to be modern and revolutionary turns out simply to support the general ideological status quo under bourgeois society; whereas some artists who adopt conventional forms may in fact be revolutionary in impact.[9]

Historical Materialism and the Arts

We know that control of the ideological superstructure of a society is crucial to the dominance of the rulers. If people did not share a consensus on norms and values, force would continually have to be applied in order that the dominant class maintain its rule. This of course is precisely what happens during crises of capitalist society. (In Canada, the Winnipeg General Strike or the Conscription Crisis in Quebec are historical examples). In some societies, particularly the countries of Europe where Communist and socialist parties are powerful, the dominant ideology of monopoly capitalism appears to be less widely accepted among the working class than in North America. What structural-functionalists would call an "institutional failure" or "dysfunction" in those societies has been rectified in ours. In North America, the institutions most important to the ideology (norms, values and beliefs) of society appear to be particularly monolithic: they are especially efficient in propagating competition, individualism, consumerism, fatalist apathy, and a rather apathetic and cynical belief in parliamentary democracy as the best political system (sometimes presented in Canada as the least among evils).

Among the institutions most important in forming ideology, it is easy to see how the educational and the popular media constitute parts of the ideological superstructure which the directing class can control quite directly and through which it can impose the values of the status quo. Historical materialism views the arts as an essential part of the ideological structure; and further it sees the arts both reflecting social change and acting as agents of change. For some of the best known Marxist thinkers such as Christopher Caudwell, Georg Lukacs and Lucien Goldmann, the study of art forms is central to their interpretation of historical and social development. The arts differ from other components of the ideological superstructure, however, in that they have *relative autonomy*: they are not as clearly and entirely regulated by the dictates of the dominant ideology as educational institutions and the popular media. This also helps to account for the keen interest of historical materialists, from Marx and Engels, right up to the present in art; for if it is not directly controlled by the exigencies of the dominant class, it has the potential of a revolutionary social role by directly or indirectly motivating the non-owners towards changing the class structure and the capitalist economic base on which it rests.

The reason for which art and literature maintain relative autonomy is that they are mediated, they are open to interpretation by the public. They cannot be as clear-cut as other expressions of ideology, so that it is not immediately certain whether they are supportive of the most important features of the dominant ideology (within capitalist society, liberalism). Therefore, their subjection to the same conditions of production, distribution and ownership as other goods which are thrown onto the capitalist market does not entirely prevent them from expressing opposition to that society from the individual point of view of the artist. Secondly, although art is subject to these conditions of the capitalist market, it does have a *cognitive* function: in teaching people something about society, art gives them some of the conceptual tools with which to start marking changes.

> While according to the ideological conception the artist addresses himself to reality in order to express his vision of the world, as well as of his time and class, the conception of art as cognition recognizes that the artist is approaching reality. The artist approaches reality to capture its essential features, to reflect it, but without dissociating his artistic reflection from his attitude to reality, that is, from the ideological content of the work. In that sense, art is a means of cognition.... (Vasquez: p. 29)

Thus we have seen, for example, that although Balzac was a conservative, a monarchic legitimist, this is transcended through the realism of his work: what stands out is a realistic portrayal of a declining artistocracy in a new bourgeois order. Similarly, as Lenin declares, Tolstoy's mysticism could not prevent his work from allowing the Russian working-class to know more about its enemies.[10]

It therefore appears that there are two sides to the historical materialist analysis of the arts. One side recognizes it as part of the ideological superstructure which helps the dominant class maintain its rule. It analyses, as for other ideological forms, the means by which this class imposes its ideology through art and literature. In feudal society, this meant the analysis of the role of the Church monopoly. For capitalist society, it means the analysis of private control over the market system. At least one well-known literary sociologist, Robert Escarpit,[11] had concentrated exclusively on this aspect, especially on the social situation of the writer. "Patronage and the costs of production replace the literary text as the centre of discussion. Thus the writer's relationship with his patron is traced in some detail, from the patronage of the medieval courts to that of eighteenth-century aristocracy. With the rise of cheap publishing and a mass market the patronage system gives way to the autocracy of the publisher and booksellers" (Laurenson and Swingewood: p. 18). Related to this problem of production and consumption is that of the situation of the writer in mass society.

> The writer's position in a mass society is extremely important as a contrast to his earlier social situation, and clearly likely to affect his creative potential in many ways; the links between this historical background and the development of literature constitutes a key area in any literary sociology. It involves two major problems, namely the precise linkage between the text and its background – how do literary production and consumption affect the form and the content of particular literary works? . . . A persistent theme of this particular sociological approach is the emphasis on the increasing alienation of the writer from his society and the consequent impact on literary style of content. (Laurenson: p. 18)

This theme has been that of the great English Marxist critic Christopher Caudwell.[12] He shows clearly, through historical analysis, the increasing alienation of British writers and the rise of art for art's sake and "modernism" as a function of the growth of bourgeois society. Note that historical materialist analysis, in emphasizing the conditions of production and distribution, focusses on writers who represent their times and not necessarily those who are considered the best.

The second side of the historical materialist approach to the social study of art and literature is based more on the recognition of that relative autonomy of the arts which gives it the possibility of "changing people's consciousness" against the dominant ideology; either because the writer is doing so unknowingly (Balzac) or because the work does not appear on the surface to challenge the general status quo – or even because a large enough number of people are committed to the kind of change which is expressed by the writer. It is therefore not so much the conditions under which the work was produced – the social, class, and ideological situation of the writer that counts – but rather its actual, long-term, objective impact. This approach, then, will focus on analysis of the literary text itself. But unlike the positivist method which treats the literary work simply as a document from which data about the society can be gathered for its own sake, the historical materialist treatment of the text will concentrate upon the impact of it in showing the processes of social change. The method becomes dynamic and dialectical when it also demonstrates how great authors can expedite fundamental social change. In writing and analyzing changes already in process, they accelerate changes still more. Thus, for Georg Lukacs, one of the foremost literary sociologists,[13] great literature creates comprehensive "human types" which, in realistically reflecting the social groups and classes of their time, show, in their interaction, the process of social change in a personalized way.

Focussing as it does on the text itself this side of historical materialist analysis will be able to distinguish between those works which are socially most significant and those which are not. It will also be able to posit a relationship between social content and aesthetic values in art and literature. Works which are socially most significant will be those of cognitive value, they will teach the reader something about social structure and about the process of change in a way which is extricably bound up with immense aesthetic impact. In doing so, the writer will be wittingly or unwittingly pointing the way toward social change. The great writer is revealed by this method to be a *social realist*, someone who artistically depicts social reality through his characters.

Social realism to the historical materialist in no way implies "documentary realism" or "naturalism" – that is the "snapshot" of the empiro-positivist, hopelessly attempting to describe everything in detail and leading only to a description of part of the observable. Change comes from analysis of what underlies the observable; so that realist art and literature can be defined as "all art that, starting with the existence of an objective reality (like social structure) constructs a new reality which gives us truth about concrete men who live in a given society, in historically and socially conditioned human relationships within which they work, struggle, suffer, rejoice or dream" (Vazquez; p. 33). We can see immediately why such literature, deriving as it does from a structural understanding of economic and social relationships, should generally be preferred by historical materialists. It is because such literature, in Canadian society for example, will show the commercialization of human relationships by the capitalist market system. But it will also show the objective opposition by the non-owners to this state of affairs, and therefore the possibility of change collectively generated through awareness of class contradictions and subsequent social movements. Contrast this with the fatalistic attitude consequent on strictly depicting the observable; with the apathy and individualism consequent upon an idealism or romanticism which does not understand the structural considerations; with the neurosis and withdrawal consequent on a modernism which considers that that the individual's isolation prevents him from joining with others in promoting change. It should also be noted that the social realist, starting from a basis of structural understanding of underlying economic determinants of social reality, has an advantage in terms of the aesthetic values in his work. The naturalist, like the positivist, is limited by what he can directly see. The idealist, like a ship wandering in a fog, does not know where to throw the anchor, because his work is not tied to any but the most subjective understanding; his writing is therefore often aimless, haphazard. The social realist, on the other hand, has an infinite number of ways in which aesthetically to demonstrate his social understanding with sensitivity and humanity.

The use of the textual method of historical materialist analysis in literature has been the approach of Lucien Goldmann.[14] It has enabled him to concentrate on the most important writers of various epochs, those who reflect the world view of significant social groups or classes and who therefore show us the historical process.

> The mediocre writer merely reflects the historical period and his work has only documentary value. But great literature tackles the major problems and it achieves its inner unity because only the 'exceptional' individual, the truly great writer, identifies with the fundamental social tendencies of his time in a way which allows him to achieve coherent expression of reality – the average writer, the average member of a group, will also grasp the social tendencies but in a confused and vague manner. (Laurenson and Swingewood: p. 68)

Goldmann's dialectical method combines beautifully the historical framework in which the writer is placed and the notion of both the literary work and the society which it portrays as totalities.

> His method, which he calls 'generalized genetic structuralism' (historical structuralism) seeks firstly to identify certain structures within particular texts, and secondly, to relate them to concrete historical and social conditions, to a social group and social class associated with the writer and to the world vision of that class. The emphasis throughout is on the text itself as a whole and on history as a process. Goldmann's approach is to extrapolate from the social group and the text under analysis an abstraction, that is, a world vision, which then becomes a working model. He turns to the text seeking to explain the whole, that is, their structures, by reference to his model. In essence, the method is a continual oscillation between texts, social structure (social groups and classes), and the model, between abstractions and the concrete, Marx's 'pre-given, living, concrete whole'. (Laurenson and Swingewood, p. 68)

For Goldmann, although he does not, like Lukacs and Marx, concentrate on social realists as the most significant writers, important writers are not those who express simply their own individualized alienation, but those who express the world vision of whole groups or classes.[15] The others are of passing, not enduring interest. If we accept this perspective, it will, together with the quest for social realism, give us a framework not only to evaluate the sociological importance of the various literary schools and works in Canada, but will also help us to understand how much significance each has in promoting social change in this country.

Notes to General Introduction: Part A

1. An important variation of this position is the contention that, in North American society and other "democracies," a tiny minority does *not* hold power.

2. For example the "Blishen scale" of describing strata, named after the Canadian sociologist Bernard Blishen.

3. Porter and Clement have in fact established that there is very little downward mobility from the Canadian corporate elite.

4. See Arnold Hauser, *Social History of Art* (London: Routledge and Kegan Paul, 1968).

5. H. Taine, "History of English Literature" quoted in Laurenson and Swingewood's *The Sociology of Literature.*

6. Kenneth Clark, "Art and Society" in M. C. Albrecht, et al. (eds.) *Sociology of Art and Literature* (New York: Praeger, 1970), p. 635

7. This, of course, is exactly what Taine and his followers have done.

8. Leo Johnson has found that fewer than 11% of Canadian income earners own as much as one share. See Leo Johnson's "The Development of Class in 20th Century Canada," in Gary Teeple's *Capitalism and the National Question in Canada* (Toronto: University of Toronto Press, 1972).

9. The famous nineteenth-century French author Balzac is often quoted by historical materialists as a writer whose beliefs were reactionary, whose literary form was fairly conventional, but whose materialist analysis is objectively akin to Marxism.

10. I.VI. Lenin, "Party Organization and Party Literature," in *Selected Works* (New York: International Publishers, 1967).

11. Robert Escarpit, *Sociologie de la Littérature* (Paris: Presses Universitaires de France, 1968).

12. Christopher Caudwell, *Illusion and Reality* (New York: International Publishers, 1973) and *Studies and Further Studies in a Dying Culture* (London and New York: Monthly Review Press, 1971).

13. Georg Lukacs, *The Historical Novel, Studies in European Realism, The Meaning of Contemporary Realism, Essays on Thomas Mann,* etc.

14. Lucien Goldmann, *The Hidden God,* translated by P. Thody (London: Routledge and Kegan Paul, 1964). Also, *Pour une Sociologie du Roman* (Paris: Gallimard, 1965) and "The Sociology of Literature" in M. C. Albrecht's *The Sociology of Art and Literature* (New York: Prager, 1970).

15. See especially *The Hidden God.*

GENERAL INTRODUCTION PART B:

TOWARDS A SOCIOLOGY OF ENGLISH CANADIAN LITERATURE

PAUL CAPPON

A sociology of English Canadian literature based on historical materialism will analyze the relationship between its writing and its total social structure. It will be an activist sociology, oriented towards showing the kinds of writing which promote social change and the kinds which retard it. It will not view our literature as simply another way to document society, nor just as the expression of the individuality of various writers. Instead, it will seek to identify essential structures of Canadian society and pose the specific problems which literature must undertake in helping to change them. Eventually, it will criticize writers in terms of the impact which their writing has on changing society rather than on subjective aesthetic values in isolation.

The relationship between literature and art and the total social structure is determined, as we have seen, by the role which they play in forming ideology. The imposition of values and norms of the ideology of the directing class is one way by which it exercises social control. The literature which dominates a society will reflect those values; but to the extent that some of it it does not because of its relative autonomy, literature can be crucial in giving people the consciousness necessary for the formation of social movements.

The chief features of the present Canadian social structure are dominated by the interrelationship between the Canadian and American capitalist classes in the continuous development of the monopoly phase of capitalism. Most of the Canadian bourgeoisie is directly dependent on its American counterpart.[1] This part of the Canadian bourgeoisie includes that sector which manges American capital and that sector (mainly in the service sector – transportation, banks, insurance companies etc.) which relies on the security of American investment for its profits. (In fact, all sectors of the Canadian bourgeoisie interlock.) This growing American control as the monopoly phase unfolds is crucial when one considers the situation of the Canadian writer, the conditions of production and distribution. Even the third sector of the Canadian bourgeoisie – independent Canadian businesses outside the service sector – shares a common interest with the other sectors and with the American bourgeoisie, that of maintaining the dominant ideology of North American capitalism. It seems apparent that national sovereignty without fundamental change in Canada's class structure is impossible because of the convergence of the joint dominant class.

In this integrated whole – a developing monopoly capitalism founded on deepening colonization of Canada – the ideological role of both the arts and of social scientific thinking is important. As long as Canadian literature displays values and modes of thought like apathy, anti-collectivism and withdrawal, it helps to atomize individuals and to impede the growth of social movements and change. By the same token, as long as liberal social science prevails, especially in the form of empiricism, it objectively supports the status quo.

An activist Canadian sociology of literature therefore takes as its first task to show the ways by which the liberal American social scientific tradition has come to dominate in Canada and to prevent its implantation in the study of literature from a social perspective. American cultural dominance has been a natural and well-documented result[2] of deepening economic penetration and of the total comtemporary Canadian social structure which is its result. Similarly, social scientific thinking, as part of the same complex, has come to be dominated by American liberalism. The fact that Canadian universities have become farm-teams or escape-homes for thousands of American academics is the result, rather than the cause, of the dominance of American liberal social science. The cause lies more in the fact that the ideological bases on which American liberal social science are founded are precisely those which suit the interests of the joint American-Canadian bourgeoisie in the exercise of social control. The kind of partial analysis which American empiricism conducts, when applied here, prevents us from studying Canadian society as an integrated whole whose inequalities, political system and cultural dependence are tied together with American imperialism.

The empiricism of partial analysis leads to the studying of different phenomena, institutions and processes separately and in isolation, even though a global analysis will reveal their interconnectedness in the Canadian-American class system. The totality of the social structure is broken up by American liberalism operating in Canada into a proliferation of subfields, thereby making it extremely difficult to obtain the kind of structural understanding necessary to change society. The study of political parties is treated separately from the study of capitalist economics and the class system. Capitalist economics itself is not taught as such, but is broken up into so many subfields that the essential structure and basis for exploitation is passed over. Literature and art are seen as separate from the society in which they are created, so that their social significance is diminished.

An analytical rather than a descriptive social science, just like the realist rather than the idealist literature, undermines the status quo by giving people the tools to understand their collective situation. For this reason it is dangerous to the dominant class; for this reason, the organization of universities into isolated sub-branches and departments on the American model is effective in barring a threat to the dominant ideology from the Canadian social sciences. In this book, the identification of the problems of Canadian literature as it relates to fundamental social structure unites the two fields in a way which should make a little clearer the ways in which it can promote social change and demystify the content of that literature.

Before proceeding to identify three of the major problems of Canadian literature as it relates to the global social structure, it is useful to show the contrasting results of the use of the empirical and the historical materialist approaches in Canadian painting. This will give a good indication of the kind of sociology of literature which we must develop.

A typical example of empiro-positivist methods as applied to Canadian art may be found in Dennis Reid's *A Concise History of Canadian Painting*. Reid's book may best be criticized in contrast to Barry Lord's *History of Canadian Painting: Toward a People's Art*, written from an historical materialist perspective. Reid's empirical work becomes a collection of notes, observations, or, at best, empirical studies of individual painters and schools. There is no central theme. The lack of any continuity based on structural analysis does not allow us to gain any sense of the significance of Canada's artistic trends and periods. Since Reid assigns no specific value or content to Canadian art, one wonders why we should bother to study it at all. If the objective in writing such a book is to affirm the value of Canadian art, this cannot be done without going beyond the value of individual painters or schools. This value cannot refer only to abstract human universals. It must refer to the specific nature of the Canadian situation from which the painters come. Thus for example, native painting is not included in this or in other standard histories of Canadian art because there is absent from these histories the theme of successive colonization and exploitation from one regime to the next. As a result, native art becomes a sub-field of Canadian art, the specialized field of some anthropologists. In general, the whole field of the social analysis of art is sub-divided many times, thereby impeding any development of ideas of historico-social continuity – like colonial exploitation. Thus the empiricist approach is not just a theoretical position. It is also the result of the whole structure of intellectual thinking in Canada as reflected in the organization of universities. Universities are organized in Canada along the American model of sub-division or fields. In making for partial and empirical analysis, this system acts as the educational structure through which the directing class exercises ideological control. Academics who wish to succeed are encouraged to take approaches which will yield immediate publishable results – the descriptive, empirical approach which can help them to promotions via an impressive curriculum vitae. At the same time, it impedes persons from taking a "cross-disciplinary" approach which might show thematic unity.

The empiricist method, whether taken from the side of aesthetics or of social science, by its nature treats individual artists or schools as separate problems. It therefore cannot treat Canadian art globally, as an understandable entity based on concrete social reality. The method therefore does not allow us to establish general conceptions of Canadian art on which to *ground* case studies. The study remains a collection of relatively isolated hypotheses or descriptions. Even if the volume of studies on Canadian art and literature of this empiricist kind grows, our understanding may not – it may even be stunted in the confusion.

Barry Lord on the other hand takes Canadian art in its social and aesthetic implications and highlights its continuity. He begins from the historical materialist position that art at all times reflects specific relations of production, and within these, a particular historical situation. In the context of Canada this implies study based on the specific nature of the different types of colonial dominance at each stage of Canada's history (French, British, American); so that the anti-imperialist struggle is highlighted. This position gives some sense to the overall evolution and significance of Canadian art: we are not studying it because it is Canadian, but because it has a *specific* significance, a characteristic content. Specific artists and schools of artists may then be related to the overall significance, the general theme of successive colonial regimes. We are given a theoretical basis and general analysis on which to ground specific examination of artists or schools. Historical continuity in the development of Canadian art is achieved by this method, and a specific significance or value is placed on Canadian art. It is not a question of searching for the expression only of universal problems in our art. Instead, it is the problem of the social content of the art of an identifiable people in a unique historical and social context.

We can therefore speak of *traditions*[3] in Canadian art insofar as artists and patrons respond to a comprehensible historical and social evolution in ways which correspond to a pattern. The establishment of traditions in turn enables us to situate artists, schools, past and future directions. Finally, this global analysis, through the correctness of its basic theme, allows us to identify errors of specific analysis, not only of others, but also within Lord's own work.[4]

It must be noted that, even when American empiricism is rejected as a method for the study of Canadian art or literature the values of liberal ideology may still dominate the analysis, and lead to a mystification of reality. The idealism of Margaret Atwood's *Survival* is the most prominent example we have so far in Canadian literary critique.[5] Atwood plays the common liberal trick of *psychologizing* social phenomena – in this case American imperialism. American dominance for her becomes something purely cultural and abstract. For her, *individuals* react to it by being victimized, but the more enlightened ones can resist it *individually* and become "creative non-victims". Solutions are therefore on the artistic-literary level and obviously only for an elite among which she clearly counts herself. The rest are too stupid or too passive to take on her anti-Americanism. Atwood's solutions to an American dominance which is in fact *material* (economic), not abstract, are those of individualism and elitism, characteristics which conform to the dominant ideology. What therefore appears to be radical because of its bitter anti-Americanism turns out in fact to be a kind of middle-class nationalism.

Atwood ends up with middle-class nationalism because her idealism corresponds to an incorrect assessment of what actually are the problems of Canadian literature. Her analysis is non-historical and anti-materialist. She therefore cannot even know for example, that the bourgeois nationalism of John A. MacDonald's National Policy only encouraged further American branch-plant penetration. Her neglect of the conomic or material basis for American dominance cannot lead to solutions on the economic level – and these are the only solutions for the collectivity. Her wrathful idealism and elitism therefore represents a mere game for the directing class.

What is important to learn from Atwood in the formulation of an activist sociology of Canadian literature is that it is not simply an anti-colonial attitude that is requisite. One must also use a materialist framework in an historical context in order to identify the real problems of Canadian literature as it relates to social change – and especially, to anti-colonialism. The rest of this introductory essay will only begin to outline three of the most important of these problems.

Patronage and Publishing

We have earlier noted the debate among historical materialists concerning the relative importance of textual analysis on the one hand and the analysis of the conditions of production and distribution on the other. Sociologists like Lukacs and Goldmann concentrated on the literary text, hoping to show the relationship between the world view of the writer and a particular social group, class or historical process. In the case of Lukacs and Caudwell social realism is considered to be the socially most progressive art form, because, by containing an implicit analysis of social structure underlying human behaviour, it gives the public cognitive tools to help social change. Other sociologists such as Escarpit have emphasized the aspect of patronage and publishing as most significant because they shape the situation of the artist. In the Canadian context, we have argued, both kinds of analysis are necessary for a full understanding of the social content of literary production.

Concentration on textual analysis assumes a relative autonomy from the dominant ideology significant enough that writers can actually be found who will express counter-ideas. In Canada this presumes that it is possible to produce an anti-colonial literature, a literature of struggle against present social structure, a literature which does not express the norms of dominant liberal individualism. Given the system of production and distribution of literature in Canada, the possibility of such a literature arising is by no means self-evident. It is therefore the first task of a sociology of Canadian literature to examine the prevailing system of patronage and publishing, in the hope that such analysis will ultimately lead to a socially activist literature.

The problem of patronage and publishing for an activist Canadian literature is based on the economic. As monopoly capitalism expands, the quantity of its surplus (profits) also grows, so that it is forever in search of new wider markets. At the same time, the continuous exacerbation of the tendency towards monopoly means that capital will concentrate more and more in fewer corporations. These two tendencies taken together make the swallowing up of both Canadian publishing houses and the Canadian market a *natural* result of monopoly capitalist expansion past national boundaries. Indeed, the homogenization of cultures can only be to the advantage of huge multi-nationals seeking expanded markets. Under normal capitalist market conditions, Canadian publishers cannot produce as cheaply as their American counterparts because the latter have the far bigger market which allows them to enjoy economies of scale. This economic phenomenon thus determines the process of homogenization on the cultural level; and the two interact and support each other in an ever-widening vicious circle of economic control and cultural dominance.

The only possibility for a relatively autonomous Canadian literature (and culture) under these conditions would be public intervention to disrupt the normal processes of developing monopoly capitalism as they apply to culture. But it is difficult to intervene in this way. The close association of the Canadian and American bourgeoisie prohibits the Canadian government from doing this. In the end, the Canadian government may only make token gestures, as it did in the cases of *Time* and *Reader's Digest*. The Canadian bourgeosie has too large a stake in monopoly capitalist development to allow it seriously to be challenged on even the cultural level. Such a challenge would set dangerous precedents for all other fields within Canadian society.

We therefore find that it is essentially the economic system which determines foreign control over distribution. The class structure associated with the economic system and the political institutions based on it make for foreign control. Finally, the ideological constructs based on the interests of the Canadian elite in this whole system prohibit massive intervention. Moreover, even when Canadians do control some of the organs of distribution or production, the influence of American liberalism is so pervasive that the work which they encourage may not be markedly more activist or even "Canadian." This is because, as we have seen, the whole intellectual and humanist organization in Canada as represented by universities and the various granting agencies is based on liberal assumptions. We have already shown how liberal values affect the work of a Reid or an Atwood. It is even more obvious how they affect artistic and literary production through a National Gallery, Canada Council, or university.

All these institutions are Canadian. Yet they function in a way that does not encourage activist Canadian art and literature because, as public institutions under governmental control, they are dominated by the proponents of liberal ideology. Most artists and writers are almost completely dependent on these institutional bulwarks of liberal ideology. In painting, for example: "It is not unusual to find artists who seldom exhibit and virtually never sell their work, perpetually applying for yet another grant to produce more work (Lord: p. 168). In literature:

> For all the good it has undoubtedly done, the Canada Council represents the final boxing-in of Canadian literature by the structure of institutionalism. If we try to envisage an "average Canadian writer", we can see him living near a campus, teaching at least part-time at the university level... and always hoping for a Canada Council fellowship." (Woodcock: p. 3)

Being largely under the control of these institutions means for the writer and the artist subjection to the "international standards" and styles which are the hallmark of liberalism – for if liberalism accepts "art for art's sake," if it does not accept as a primary objective of art the fostering of social change in the milieu in which it was produced, then arts grounded specifically in Canadian problems will have no special value. Liberalism in this sense implies the kind of "internationalism" which claims in the universities that partial analysis and empiricism are universal and scientific; and which allows power in granting institutions to Americans and British, who allegedly know and understand these international standards best. In fact, the use of "international standards," for specific Canadian problems is simply the ideological and cultural side of the coin of economic domination. Thus Lord writes:

> The Director of the Montreal Museum of Fine Arts and the Chief Curator of the Art Gallery of Ontario, are just two examples of U.S. citizens at prominent posts. The art history departments of our English-speaking universities and the art departments of our colleges and universities are [also] among the most heavily dominated by U.S. and British professors.[6] Even the editor of *Artscanada*, the 'national art magazine' is an American. (Lord: p. 161)

What is important, as Lord points out, is not that persons holding these influential posts are foreigners, but that they, like Canadian academics and cultural bureaucrats "are convinced that all good modern and contemporary art comes from New York." Lord demonstrates the complex interlocking of the cultural bureaucracy in Canada with American cultural institutions and dealers, American capitalists like the Carnegie and Rockefeller interests, and the Canadian bourgeoisie;[7] the whole relationship resulting in the subjection of Canadian artists to the "international standards" and styles which represent the passive acceptance of the general social status quo, under American-dominated monopoly capitalism.

> Exhibitions, purchases, lectures and publications (of the National Gallery and Canada Council) presented one unanimous continentalist opinion; cultural bureaucrats agreed with comprador collectors, and encouraged petit-bourgeois patrons like doctors and lawyers to think and buy the same way. Instead of providing a bastion for our national culture as Massey had intended, government patronage systematically promoted our dependence on the U.S.A. (Lord: p. 198)

In literature the situation is similar. It is difficult for writers to conquer the American market if they base their writings on activist criticism specific to the Canadian social structure. Consequently, Canadian writers who are published by branch-plant publishing houses are likely to have adopted the "international" styles or content which diminish their social value here. If they try the other route – through the application for grant money from institutions like the Canada Council – they will often have to conform to the same kinds of standards. The granting agency, before giving money, seeks the opinion of the "experts," who are usually associated with universities. But since we have seen that these are likely to share the liberal, continentalist view in the humanities as in the social sciences, it would be difficult for a large volume of activist Canadian literature to be produced. As Milton Acorn says of such people in his poem "England":

> Trained to administer colonies, they discover with surprise
> There're so few colonies left the competition
> Is so fierce it's like a river full of crocodiles –
> No other edible beast in sight:
> So they come to Canada and other naive places
> To administer the colonies of the American Empire.

The problem of the production and distribution of activist Canadian literature then does not depend only on the existence of Canadian publishing houses or on public institutional support. These will give rise at best to an Atwoodian middle-class nationalism unless some control over them is exercised by those who wish to go beyond having Canadian literature being produced simply because it is Canadian. For this kind of intervention, changes are required in the ideological system and its economic and institutional supports seen as a totality.

Social Realism and a Language of Struggle

The relative popularity of poets like Dorothy Livesay and Milton Acorn or of novelists like Phillip Grove and Margaret Laurence demonstrates that the problem of patronage and publishing has not entirely prevented a realist literature of struggle from developing.[8] Even in a society so heavily dominated by American liberal ideology, Canadian literature has always maintained a relative autonomy. Contrary to Atwood's claim, there has always been collective resistance to bourgeois social structures and to American domination. Even in the 1930's there were literary tabloids developing a language of struggle; like *Masses* or *New Frontier*. In New Frontier, Norman Bethune had written at the time of the Spanish Civil War: "The function of the artist is to disturb. His duty is . . . to shake the complacent pillars of the world . . . In a world terrified by change he preaches revolution – the principle of life. He is an agitator, a disturber of the peace. . . . He is the creative spirit working in the soul of man."[9]

If it is true that activist literature is and has always been produced in this country, there remains some reason to distinguish the social content and impact of the various writers.[10] In other words, textual analysis, as well as the problems of patronage, remains important for the sociology of Canadian literature because what some writers say – and the influence they have – will be more socially significant than others. The second major problem of the sociology of Canadian literature therefore would be similar to that of Goldmann or Lukacs: to identify writers who do represent the world view of an important collectivity and to discover those who, through their writing, teach us something about our society.

Many of our writers have sought idealistic retrenchment.[11] A sociology of literature must relate this phenomenon to its social basis. Idealism, as we have seen with Atwood, implies an individualism which cuts the writer off from his social milieu and so prevents him from becoming an effective agent of a collectivity. It is rooted in a lack of understanding of his own society or in a fundamental apathy about collectively-induced change. Even when social change is envisaged, as in Hugh MacLennan's depiction of Canada's becoming a nation in *Barometer Rising*, the idealist tends to psychologize or individualize social phenomena[12] which are, in reality, founded in concrete economic and political trends. More often, however, idealism leads to alienated, modernistic writers like Leonard Cohen, who see themselves and others as isolated individuals.

The social basis for idealist retrenchment and modernism in Canadian literature seems to be essentially the atomization of individuals within middle-class society. Everyone has to "make it on their own" because freedom is essentially individual – and this is the main feature of liberal ideology. The modernistic, idealist novel then must be seen as largely a function of Canadian capitalist society, not simply as the result of the particular personality of the writer. That personality is formed in a distinct and socially defined framework.

The rootless nature of Canadian modernist and idealist literature is exacerbated by the nature of Canadian monopoly capitalist society as increasingly dominated by the U.S. imperial centre. We have seen that, within a liberal framework in which tastes have nothing to do with social content ("art for art's sake"), the main criterion for success will be the adaptation of current imperial styles. But style and content are very much related; so that the Canadian writer who adopts imported forms will be unlikely to base his writing on anything which is socially specifically pertinent to his Canadian context. Uprooted in this way, he will be most likely to feel, think and write in much the mood and style of the imperial centre. If, as is now the case, that mood and style is that of the alienated modernist, textual analysis of this kind of writing will reveal little that is of social significance over the long term. It simply reflects the mood in the imperial centre at a given time. It would not reflect, in the sense of Goldmann, the world view of any important group or class in Canadian society.

The second mainstream of writing that textual analysis of Canadian literature in its social perspective may reveal is one of documentary realism. Lord defines documentary realism as "the practice of recording social reality as the artist finds it, with the artist preferring the discipline of his observed subject matter to any stylistic concern." (Lord: p. 101) Emile Zola is usually described as one of the greatest writers who would fit this category. In Canada, Irene Baird's 1938 novel *Waste Heritage* may serve as an example. In this country, documentary realism would probably gain currency as a form during times in which a generalized consensus on social injustice already existed. The 1930's is an obvious example in Canada as in the United States; and in some ways Baird is comparable with Steinbeck. The writer is encouraged to depict social malfunctions in detail only, to repeat, when a consensus already exists on those malfunctions. While documentary realists describe reality, however, they would not go so far as to show the kind of analysis which would get at the root of the malfunction – capitalist society itself. It is significant in this respect that documentary realists like Baird are generally drawn from a petite bourgeoisie which, its own security threatened by the crisis, is sympathetic with the oppressed working class; but the writer is only a sympathetic observer, she is not of the working class, nor does she identify with it.

Social realism, a third mainstream of Canadian literature which can be identified by textual analysis, *does* have its roots in the working class. This does not mean that the writer must come from that class; but that he must have in mind the large-scale social change which will destroy the dominance of the bourgeoisie, or that the writer, even without consciously sharing that perspective, objectively gives the public cognitive tools with which to promote social change. Balzac in nineteenth-century France and possibly Margaret Laurence in contemporary Canada are novelists who unconsciously contribute to social change through their realism. Phillip Grove is a Canadian writer who did it consciously.

Lord's definition of social realism is an exaggerated one but it does make the main point:

> Social realism is art that serves the people: it reveals the underlying contradictions in the world, lays bare the class struggle that is going on in society, and takes up the side of the working class and the oppressed. It gives confidence and courage to those engaged in the fight. It is definitely an art of fight, not plight. (Lord: p. 189)

Social realism is therefore akin to historical materialism in its analytic character, attempting to get at what underlies social appearances, the better to make for social change. Its social basis is in its representation of the interests of those who are not members of the dominant class – the working class and the collective-worker component of the middle class. Because of its orientation towards far-reaching change in the economic and social structure and its support to workers in the class struggle, this literature may be said, in the Goldmann sense, to represent the world view of an important social group.

The critical difference between the usual presentation of documentary realists and that of social realists, as mentioned by Lord, is that the latter are not content simply to show the "plight of the workers" in all its pessimism; for the reality is that workers are not isolated: they constitute a potential unity as a class struggling against the directing class. To show that workers are not without hope, that the people constitute a collectivity in opposition to bourgeois rule is to demonstrate that isolation and alienation are not the necessary human condition. It shows that, given the tools of knowledge and collective consciousness, change can be produced in the social sphere and in the individual's relationship with society.[13]

Grove's novel *The Master of the Mill* is an example of a social realist novel. It shows clearly the relationship between economic structure and social behaviour. Grove's characters are conditioned by their class affiliation, they do not act randomly. The capitalistic protagonist of the novel acts against his humanist instinct but as his class role dictates, echoing the general development of bourgeois society as a mockery of its original egalitarian ideals. He is forced into an ever greater rationalization of production and consequent increased rate of exploitation of his mill workers. At the same time, the workers also behave as workers. They are not idealized or romanticized; nor is their "plight" exaggerated. Indeed, we are left with the feeling that they may yet act collectively for a change in the economic system and the class structure.

The master of the mill, on the other hand, cannot participate in the active formulation of a new type of society as long as he retains his class position – which he finds it impossible to abandon. Like any good social realist writer, Grove depicts the capitalist with human understanding: the problem is fundamentally a structural problem of class relations, not that of the personality of an individual capitalist. In reality, capitalists are not villains as individuals, so that social realism will not show them as such.

Social realist literature need not deal in every novel or play with the whole range of the class struggle directly. Indeed, as Laurence's work shows, it need not even be mentioned explicitly. Social realism need not be dramatic to be effective, or even seem to deal with larger issues like class or social movement. Nevertheless, in depicting aesthetically one or more aspects underlying social structure as they relate to the totality of social organization – whether it be the situation of Canadian women or the results of imperialism, social realism contributes to the breaking down of the dominant ideology by showing the real world without mystification.

There is a potential for social realist literature even given the ideological constraints of Canadian society. It may be that the development of a language of struggle against imperialism and for social change does not imply anything more than a real, deep structural understanding of Canadian society by our writers, the kind of understanding reflected in social realism.[14] Textual analysis of the content of English Canadian writing as it relates to social organization will reveal the extent to which that understanding and that language are developing.

Regional Literature in Canada

A third problem basic to a sociology of Canadian literature is that of regionalism.[15] The identification of Canada's literature as a whole as "regional" is an extension of the economic and social reality of Canada's situation of "hinterland" to first the British then the American "metropolis." We have seen how this reality is fundamental to the problems both of patronage and publishing and of the ideological influences of American liberalism as reflected in Canadian literary texts. Through the metropolis-hinterland reality, are therefore related the three major problems of a nascent sociology of Canadian literature. An activist sociology will thus be clearly connected with the anti-colonial struggle through its taking up these problems.

The tendency to treat Canadian literature as regional is as deeply rooted as the application of those "international standards" which are the reflection of foreign domination. Even a perceptive critic such as George Woodcock, is sufficiently permeated with this system of literary criticism that he says in one breath: "In Canada, the factors that differentiate intellectual life from that in the rest of North America are even greater than those distinguishing one American region from another" (Woodcock: p. 139); and in the next breath that Canada's literature has "emerged as a clearly defined regional tradition. I use the word *regional* quite deliberately . . . because it emphasizes that Canadian writers belong within the greater tradition of Anglo-Saxon literature and have to establish a place there as individuals" (Woodcock: p. 140-141). While no one would argue that a writer's place may be established by anyone but himself, what Woodcock and many internationalists are saying is that Canadian writers must cut themselves off from their concrete material roots in order to meet the standards of this "greater tradition."Thus, "only a few Canadian writers who had deliberately cultivated international affiliations, like Morley Callaghan and A. J. M. Smith seemed at this time *to be able to overcome the limiting factors of the environment*" (Woodcock: p. 141, [italics mine]). This idealist position is the direct opposite of the liberating position which alone might produce a strong activist English Canadian literature.

The idealist and internationalist position, stemming from colonial dominance and that of liberal ideology, condemns Canadian literature forever to the status of "regional." It can never therefore be significant in its own right. The opposite position is that there is no such thing as *regional* Canadian writing; that all great writing must come from a firm founding on the environmental and social milieu of the writer. He must grasp the unique historical and social framework which form him and inform his work. If universal problems and values are treated, if real lasting international standing is achieved, it is *because* the writer is basing his work on the concrete social reality of his time and place – *not in spite of it*. This is analogous to the idea that only truly independent nations may become internationalist, by using their autonomy as a foundation for their internationalism. The link between an anti-imperialist struggle and the full development of Canada's literary potential therefore lies partially in the rejection of the internationalist notion of a "regional" Canadian literature. The possibility for rejection of that notion and practice, however, is bound up with the problems of patronage and publishing and of continentalist dominance in the institutions like the Canada Council and the universities which have much control over the character of the work which is produced.

The extension of the notion of regionalism *within* Canadian literature parallels and depends upon the extension of the metropolis-hinterland relationship within the satellite. Central Canada is the geographical hub through which American economic penetration dominates Canadian social reality; it therefore becomes not only the place from which art styles of the imperial centre are disseminated within the satellite, but also the originator of forms and styles which are particular to the satellite. The foundation of its dominance is, of course, essentially economic: as the financial centre with controlling interests in hinterland areas, it is also the location of publishing houses and important art institutions. Just as a painting by a B.C. artist is likely to be found in the Art Gallery in Toronto, in the National Gallery or in the Toronto Public Library, writers from the hinterland find difficulty unless they have the support of Toronto publishing houses (most of which are branch-plant) and Ontario taste-controllers.

The counter to the notion of regionalism within Canada is again the idea that good writing must reflect the social conditions and specific problems of the writers' locale, and that a particular form and style may be appropriate to the problems of a particular region. These forms and styles need not be the prevailing mode elsewhere in the country. When literature expresses a local reality in its own mode, this expression of variety can only be an advantage. It is difficult, for example, to imagine success of the Theatre Passe Muraille's *Farm Show* if it had not adopted a form which would express the social reality of south-western Ontario's farming region. At the same time, because the show's format was determined by *local* conditions, it was able to take account of *universal* problems. It could, no doubt, be understood not only across Canada but abroad.

Not *regional literature* but *literature based on regional social realities* has always flourished in the various hinterlands of Canada, as has literature of struggle associated with it. Given the objective conditions of production and distribution of literature in Canada, however, it will take a conscious effort to ensure its growth.

Notes to General Introduction: Part B

1. See James Laxer (ed.), (Canada) *Limited* (Toronto: McClelland and Stewart, 1973) for a more exhaustive analysis.

2. See Barry Lord, *History of Painting in Canada; Toward a People's Art* (*Toronto*: N.C. Press, 1974).

3. One good example of such a tradition is that of landscape painters such as the Group of Seven. Lord shows how these artists and their patrons were responding to a historical situation of the growth of a Canadian bourgeoisie and, consequently, of strong middle-class nationalism.

4. It may well be argued that there are many errors and exaggerations in Lord's book, but this does not nullify its overall achievement.

5. We need not expound here at length on Atwood's work, since it is central to other essays in this volume.

6. For a full documentation of the influence of American academics in Canadian universities (up to 1968), see Robin Mathews and James Steele, *The Struggle for Canadian Universities* (*Toronto*: New Press, 1968).

7. Examples are: Samuel Bronfman as Director of the Montreal Museum of Fine Arts; the Eaton family's dominating the board of *Artscanada* magazine; Ayala Zacks as Director of the Art Gallery of Ontario.

8. Themes of struggle which are easily assimilable or controllable have always been tolerated.

9. See also the essay by Robin Mathews in this volume, "Devoloping a Language of Struggle."

10. For an analysis of the relationship between social content, aesthetic values and techniques among Canadian writers, see Robin Endres' essay on Marxist literary critique and English Canadian literature in this volume.

11. See Endres' essay in this volume.

12. In *Barometer Rising*, it is almost as if Canada were personified.

13. Maxim Gorky, in the conclusion to his *Fragments from my Diary* expresses this beautifully and poetically:

> Whenever I have felt that such and such a truth merely slashes cruelly at the soul and teaches nothing, that it degrades a man without explaining him to me, then, of course, I have thought it better to omit it.
>
> There are, I assure you, many truths which it is best not to remember. These truths are born of lies and possess all the elements of that poisonous untruth which [has] distorted the relation of man with man.

In Introduction to Gorky's *Fragments*, M. Budberg says of Gorky's realism: "Artistic truth is more convincing than the truth of a dry fact... Gorky's realism is not a photographic one, his task is not to give a "snapshop" of reality; he organizes it in his mind and gives a picture of his own conceptions of life. Therefore there is no contradiction in his assessment of himself as a romantic. But his romanticism was in no way an idealisation of reality, it was an artist's way of rendering it." (Gorky, *Fragments from My Diary*, trans. M. Budberg (London: Penguin Books, 1972). This is true social realism.

14. In fact, *socialist* realism is much more likely to help produce radical change. *The Master of the Mill* is *social* realism in its depiction of elements underlying social structure and behaviour. It is not yet *socialist* realism because it does not show this from the viewpoint of the workers, but rather from that of the capitalist. Although this is better than the destructive idealism of middle-class novelists which pretends to represent the workers' viewpoint but ends up romanticizing or idealizing them, it is still one step removed from socialist literature.

15. See Patricia Marchak's essay on regionalism in Canadian literature in this volume.

Bibliography

Albrecht, M. C. "Art as an Institution." Albrecht, Barnett, and Griff, eds., *The Sociology of Art and Literature*. New York: Prager, 1970.

Atwood, M. E. *Survival: A Thematic Guide to Canadian Literature*. Toronto: Anansi, 1972.

Carr, E. H. *What is History?* London: Penguin Books, 1964.

Caudwell, C. *Illusion and Reality, A Study of the Sources of Poetry*. New York: International Publishers, 1967.

________, "Studies and Further Studies in a Dying Culture."New York: *Monthly Review Press*, 1971.

Clark, K. *Civilization*. London: British Broadcasting Corporation and John Murray, 1969.

________, "Art and Society." Albrecht, Barnett and Griff eds., *The Sociology of Art and Literature*. New York: Praeger, 1970.

Coser, L. *The Functions of Social Conflict*. Glencoe: The Free Press, 1956.

Escarpit, R. *Sociologie de la Littérature*. Paris: Presses Universitaires de France, 1968.

Goldmann, L. *The Hidden God*. London: Routledge and Kegan Paul, 1964.

________, *Pour une Sociologie du Roman*, Paris: Gallimard, 1965.

________, "The Sociology of Literature: Status and Problems of Methods." Albrecht, Barnett, and Griff eds., *The Sociology of Art and Literature*, New York: Praeger, 1970.

Gorsky, M. *Fragments from My Diary*. M. Budgerg, trans., London: Penguin Books, 1972.

Hauser, A. *The Social History of Art*, 4 vols., London: Routledge and Kegan Paul, 1968.

Inkeles, A. *What is Sociology?*, Englewood Cliffs: Prentice-Hall, 1964.

Johnson, L. A. "The Development of Class in Canada in the Twentieth Century," in G. Teeple ed., *Capitalism and the National Question in Canada.* Toronto: University of Toronto Press, 1972.

Jones. G. S. "History: The Poverty of Empiricism," in R. Blackburn ed., *Ideology in Social Science*, Bungay: Fontana/Collins, 1972.

Kornhauser, W. *The Politics of Mass Society*. New York: Free Press, 1959.

Laurenson, D., and Swingewood, A. *The Sociology of Literature*. London: Paladin, 1972.

Laxer, R. ed., *(Canada) Ltd.*, Toronto: McClelland and Stewart, 1973.

Lenin, V. I. "Party Organization and Party Literature." *Selected Works*. New York: International Publishers, 1967.

Lord, B. *The History of Painting in Canada: Toward a People's Art*. Toronto: N C Press, 1974.

Lukacs, G. *The Historical Novel*. London: Merlin Press, 1962.

________, *The Meaning of Contemporary Realism*. London: Merlin Press, 1963.

________, *Essays on Thomas Mann*. London: Merlin Press, 1964.

________, *Studies in European Realism*. New York: Grosset and Dunlop, 1964.

Mathews, R. and Steele, J. *The Struggle for Canadian Universities*. Toronto: New Press, 1968.

Parsons, T. and Skils, E. *Working Papers in the Theory of Action*. Glencoe: The Free Press, 1959.

Reid, D. *A Concise History of Canadian Painting*. Toronto: Oxford University Press, 1973.

Shaw, M. "The Coming Crisis of Radical Sociology." in R. Blackburn ed., *Ideology in Social Science*. Bungay: Fontana/Collins, 1972.

Taine, H. *History of English Literature*. London: Chatto and Windus, 1906.

Vazquez, A. S. *Art and Society: Essays in Marxist Aesthetics*. New York: Monthly Review Press, 1973.

Warhaft, S., ed. *Francis Bacon, A Selection of His Works*. Toronto: Macmillan, 1965.

Woodcock, G. *Odysseus Ever Returning: Essays on Canadian Writers and Writings*. Toronto: McClelland and Stewart, 1970.

PART 1: LITERARY CRITICISM IN CANADA

INTRODUCTION
PAUL CAPPON

Canadian literature had been much ignored by Canadians until a "movement" of re-discovery in the 1960's. When George Woodcock referred in his 1966 essay (Woodcock: p. 83) to Canadian literature's coming into its own, he was probably thinking as much about the readership as about the writers themselves. But he was referring also to Canadian literary critique, which, like the literature itself, has always existed – but has simply been ignored. Even the Canadian international literary celebrity, Northrop Frye, did not take up questions of Canadian literature specifically; he preferred to deal in universal kinds of mythological structures.

On this apparently quiet beach of Canadian literature and literary criticism lying like so much isolated and abandoned driftwood, Margaret Atwood's book *Survival: A Thematic Guide to Canadian Literature* broke like a huge wave, tossing things about and setting all the driftwood in motion. In Canadian terms her book was a best-selling prodigy. It was extrordinarily popular for many reasons: it struck the chord of anti-Americanism, resonant at the time; and it coincided with a general growing interest in Canadian literature. But most of all, it tried to make *overall sense* of our literature; to show that it was not just a patchwork of novels and poems of varying calibre, but that there were underlying themes relating to Canadian social life. People grasped at something which seemed to give meaning to it all. The fact that this meaning could now be connected with the problem of American cultural domination gave it immediate and obvious relevance for many Canadians.

When we come to consider the social impact and import of Canadian literary criticism and the influence which this criticism has on the literature itself, we must begin with Atwood's "survival hypothesis," even though, chronologically, it should be discussed much later. From a sociological viewpoint, Atwood's impact with *Survival* is important not only because it has been taken seriously by so many Canadians but also because it is in some ways the culmination of a tradition which has its roots much farther back than Atwood herself. James Steele's essay, "The Literary Criticism of Margaret Atwood," demonstrates this quite clearly. Steele shows how Atwood follows the idealism, cosmopolitanism and liberalism of Northrop Frye, although she appears on the surface to be the opposite – a virulent anti-American and a crusader for change. The introductory essay by Cappon in this book noted that many militant positions taken by writers are superficial and do not necessarily involve structural change. With Atwood, we see that the same is true for literary criticism: Steele reveals how Atwood's anti-Americanism, founded as it is on liberal positions, leads only to utopian individualism. Collectively generated social change is ignored or declared to be impossible.

Why then should Atwood's version of Canadian literature be so popular? One reason, as we have seen, is its superficial radicalism. Another reason, more interesting when literature and literary criticism are considered from a social perspective, is that Atwood's elitist solutions are founded on the premises of the pervasive liberal ideology in Canada. Steele shows how, by popularizing the literary critical postures of Frye and others, Atwood transmits these to her own work. Steele describes the approach of Frye and the American critic, Eric Berne, as static and ahistorical. This corresponds to the empiro-positivism in American (continentalist) social science. When Steele discusses the tendency of Berne and Frye to consider one aspect of reality in isolation (Berne's individualism and Frye's idealism), we are reminded of the splitting by liberal sociologists of the totality of social structure into various empirical units, like the semi-autonomous institutions which are the "building blocks" of Inkeles' society. In Frye's literary criticism, the autonomy of the literary universe from the social world is paralleled in structural-functional sociology by the notion of the autonomy of political and social institutions. Similarly, Steele shows how the critics Frye and Arnold wish to "transcend social class" through individual enlightenment, thereby avoiding the "anarchy" of class conflict. In structural-functionalism, this is the reduction of social conflict through regulation by equilibriating mechanisms or through its institutionalization. Individualism is inherent in structural-functionalism's notion of social mobility: in this domain also, individuals may transcend their stratum, rising to another by individual "skills" and achievement in competition with other members of society.

These similarities between the Frye/Atwood tradition of idealism and elitism in literary criticism on the one hand and American social science on the other must not be seen as mere analogies: instead, they are based on the common values, norms and beliefs of liberal ideology. Steele's essay would seem to indicate that these have dominated Canadian letters as they have Canadian social science. The irony of Atwood's literary criticism is that she provides a resume of this value sytem in a form which *looks* to be the opposite of the status quo, but is not in fact a new departure either for Canadian literary criticism or for Canadian literature. It shows simply that we have in the past and continue to be dominated by liberal ideology in Canadian arts as in social science.

A new departure for Canadian literature and literary criticism with respect to its social content and impact will therefore have to turn to theories of literature which have not been formulated within the mainstream North American tradition. Robin Endres turns to European Marxist sources to show that the literary criticism most useful for social change in Canada will be found in European dialectical materialist models of the study of literature. An overview of literary criticism which aims eventually toward more socially conscious criticism must take serious account of Marxist approaches.

In the introductory essay "Towards a Sociology of Canadian Literature," it was stated that there existed three related and immediate problems for an activist sociology of Canadian literature: the problem of regionalism; the problem of production, distribution, and the situation of the writer; and the problem of the social content and impact of individual works or schools of literature. Steele's essay deals with this latter problem from the point of view of literary criticism. Endres' essay on "Marxist Literary Criticism and English Canadian literature" begins where Steele leaves off – with literary criticism – but also moves on to the content of English Canadian literature itself.

In Endres' essay we understand how the individualism of liberal ideology as a necessary support for developing capitalism becomes in literature the expression of the "bourgeois illusion of freedom"; and Endres demonstrates how this category will help us comprehend the socio-historical development of Canadian literature. Empiro-positivism encourages an analysis based on discrete and autonomous human units. Revolutionary in its early opposition to feudal rule but finally the intellectual bulwark of capitalism, the bourgeois illusion of freedom is "a triumphant truth [the growth and increasing prosperity of capitalism], then it is a gradually revealed lie." The notion that freedom is essentially the limitation on constraints on the individual is common to both liberal social science and "mainstream" Canadian literature. This leads in both to a relativism which sees some restrictions as inevitable, therefore that a bourgeois society in which some individuals may by their isolated action gain some "freedom" may be the best solution available. In literature expressing the bourgeois illusion of freedom, the "conditions of capitalism such as poverty are projected on to all of nature as an inevitable and timeless law" (Endres): The echo of this in structural-functionalist sociology, as we find with Parsons and Inkeles, is that social stratification is part of the human condition. Only the individual, through upward mobility (liberal sociology) or through spiritual illumination (literature), may find a measure of relief.

The growth of the specific doctrines of liberal social science has not been arbitrary—it has corresponded to the intellectual attitudes necessary at the different stages of development of capitalist society. Similarly for Endres, the Caudwellian notion of the illusion of freedom does not describe literature indescriminately at every stage of bourgeois society. Instead, she makes of it a useful sociological tool by showing that the concept has taken on different meanings at different stages of Canada's economic and social development. The application of the concept thereby helps us better to understand Canadian society and ideology during the various historical periods.

Analysis of textual content will show that most well-known Canadian writers have shared the bourgeois illusion of freedom, as most Canadians are premeated by liberal ideology. Textual analysis has also revealed for Endres, however, that other writers, denied access to a wide public by the mechanisms of distribution, have adopted the Caudwellian Marxist idea that freedom is the consciousness of necessity. In the introductory essay, it is stated that it is important to recognize these writers and to account for their expression of militant opposition or counter-ideology. A crucial question also will be the relationship between the progressive social content of such works and their aesthetics. To be successful as activist literature, progressive writing must also find an appropriate form and language, integrating form and content. Endres, in discussing Livesay's poetry and Laurence's novels, shows how this can be achieved.

When Endres takes up and applies Lukacs' critique of the modernist novel in contrast to social realism she is treating another crucial part of the problem of textual analysis in the sociology of Canadian literature. Under liberal social science, just as freedom is individual and inequality part of the human condition, so is alienation essentially a psychological state not to be confused with the social structures surrounding the individual. Alienation in the workplace, for example, would be seen as a function of machine-directed labour equally observable in any capitalist of communist society where there is machine production. This position, as Endres shows, is expressed in "mainstream" Canadian literature: "The modernist sees this as an inevitable aspect of human nature." Historical materialist social scientific analysis instead gives specific definition to the alienation existing within capitalism and describes its relationship to the psychological state of solitariness.[1] Similarly, Endres points out that, in literature, "the depiction of alienation in the novel must be the result of the social context of the person who is suffering from it, and this is the case in the novel of realism."

In contrasting modernism and realism, freedom as an illusion and freedom as the recogition of necessity, Endres is contrasting the effect in literature of the opposing theoretical positions described in the introductory essay. Her textual analysis of Canadian literary works which stem from these opposing positions and from their related ideologies therefore represents an important beginning for a sociological understanding of English Canada, using literary texts as a means of understanding structures, change and ideology in this country.

Note

1. See especially the work of the Hungarian social scientist Istvan Meszaros.

THE LITERARY CRITICISM OF MARGARET ATWOOD

JAMES STEELE

The union of sociologists and literary critics is surely a welcome one for the content of Canadian literature. As a French sociologist, Lucien Goldmann, has cogently argued, the discipline of sociology should take into account certain facts of human consciousness which are to be found only in the world visions of significant literary works. Such visions can provide unique keys to an understanding of the mental structures which are charactaristics of not just individual writers but whole groups and classes of men. A corollary of this argument is that literary criticism as a human science must somehow combine both an explication of the internal coherence of literary texts with a sociological explanation of the organizing structures which provide the basis of this coherence. As virtually no criticism of this kind has been attempted in Canada by either sociologists or literary critics, any step in this direction is to be welcomed.

Nevertheless, it is with some reluctance – if not misgiving – that I write on the subject of "Margaret Atwood's survival hypothesis." It is undeniable, of course, that Atwood's theory does attempt to describe the substantial structures of Canadian literary texts and that it does try to relate these to a specific social context. It is also true that *Survival* has been widely read.

In fact, with sales now reaching some 40,000 copies, it has been more widely read than any other critical work in Canadian history. Reviewed widely and cited in both popular and learned presses, it has also found its way onto the reading lists of Canadian literature courses in both high schools and universities. In all probability, *Survival* has introduced many Canadians to their own literature for the first time. The fact remains, however, that many knowledgeable students of Canadian literature have found the "survival hypothesis" so implausible that they have had considerable difficulty in taking it seriously. To say this is not to suggest that the book has not performed a useful service. Even if one disagrees with much of Atwood's argument and even if one feels chagrined at the thought of large numbers of students entering university as militant "survivalists," it is better that Canadians should be reading their own literature for the wrong reasons than that they should be unaware of its existence. Canadian literature it could be argued, can speak for itself, and truth will surely out in the end if we take our literature as seriously as Atwood suggests we should.

Atwood herself tells her readers that there is nothing sacrosanct about her perspective: it is offered merely as a "model" which reflects her concerns as a writer while providing her with a vantage point which she finds personally satisfying. Atwood also modestly informs us that she does not try "to make her citations add up to a balanced overview of what's been written in Canada"; her primary interest is the literature of the past few decades. Nor is she concerned with the development of Canadian literature as part of an historical process. What she provides is a static dissection of its subject matter rather than a "dynamic examination of a process-in-motion," and this anatomy is meant to be suggestive rather than totally accurate. Apparently Atwood originally intended to produce a short easy-to-use guide for students and teachers who suddenly find themselves dealing with that unknown subject – Canadian Literature. But in the act of writing, the book evidently developed into something more than a mere, annotated pop bibliography: it became an attempt to outline "a number of thematic patterns which characterize the subject matter of Canadian literature." Our literature, it is argued, is essentially about the varying struggles of victims to survive victimization, and readers are nonchalantly invited to play Find-the-Victim as they go about their own reading. Only insofar as this gamesome hypothesis has been taken more seriously by Atwood's 40,000 readers than by Atwood herself, should it be regarded as something more than a critical *jeu d'esprit*.

The main reason why knowledgeable students of Canadian literature, no matter what their critical predilections, find the survival hypothesis unconvincing is that it fails to account for – or is contradicted by – too much Canadian literature. Is our literature in fact primarily about victims struggling to survive? For every citation by Atwood of a struggling victim, any reader of Canadian literature with a reasonably good memory should be able to cite at least two examples of victors who revel in success. They can be easily found in the nineteenth-century work of Goldsmith, Kirby, Sangster, Roberts and Lampman, or in the twentieth-century writings of Duncan, Leacock, Pratt, Smith, Livesay, Scott and Cohen. And, of course, both victims and victors are frequently present in the same work. In Kirby's "The U.E.: A Tale of Upper Canada," which Atwood chooses not to discuss, the poor victim, according to her paradigm, would be Ethwald, killed at Windmill Point while fighting off American guerillas. But there are victors in the poem as well – the father Walwyn and his grandson – and it could be argued that the poem is primarily about their success as British imperialists and as agents of divine providence.

Or consider Ernest Thompson Seton's stories, which Atwood does discuss. These are said to be essentially about victimization because all of Thompson Seton's animals are killed or somehow die in the end. This identification of theme with one aspect of narrative, however, is radically incomplete: what is lacking is some account of the Carlylian moral vision which is a key structural principle in most of Thompson Seton's stories. For this author celebrates again and again certain qualities of character – strength, cunning, courage, loyalty, obedience, love, self-sacrifice – which give his animal heroes security or power in a natural world which is red in tooth and claw. Atwood's cites Thompson Seton's remark in his "Preface" to *Wild Animals I Have Known* that "the life of a wild animal always has a tragic end." But Thompson Seton also asserts in that same

"Preface" that all of his animals "show the stamp of heroism and personality more strongly by far than it has been in the power...[of his] pen to tell." The "real personality of the individual and his view of life are...[his] theme." In other words, Thompson Seton's stories have to do not merely with pathetic deaths of animals but with those qualities of character which make for heroic leaders among men – qualities which reveal themselves particularly at those critical moments when the hero is faced with the ultimate struggle against death. Nobility of character is thus inherent in the haughty contempt for man shown by the dying wolf Lobo, and the silent death of the gentle partridge Redruff is marked by stoic fortitude. These moral points may not appeal to Atwood, but they were well understood by Thompson Seton's contemporaries, whose lives in a pre-monopoly, competitive, capitalist society were likewise shaped by struggle. Charles G. D. Roberts, for instance, in *The Heart of the Ancient Wood* has David teach Miranda that while life may seem "like a few butterflies flitterin' over a graveyard," life really might be "somethin' finer than the finest kind of dream." It was self-evident to them that the progress of the country depended on entrepreneurial leadership and that the essence of that leadership consisted of certain qualities of character, some of which may be discerned even in the behaviour of animals. Few contemporary readers would have agreed with the comment of the snobbish anthropologist who said in a review of *Wild Animals I Have Known* that the book deals "on nearly every page, with characteristics shared by lower animals and man – especially men of the lower culture-grades." None would have dreamed of Atwood's semi-existentialist interpretation of the animal-as-victim-in-a-meaningless-universe. From a less partial reading of Thompson Seton's animal stories, it would, indeed, be possible to construct a herological, victor-conquest theory more plausible than the victim-survival thesis, and corroborating evidence for it could be found in the work of many authors including even Atwood herself.

Atwood further supports her argument with the assertion that Canadian literature is "written almost entirely in an ironic mode and offers no worthwhile gods, no realms of romance, no divine Edens." Yet precisely these things can be found in the transcendant solace which Charles G. D. Roberts associated with the Tantramar Marshes in "Ave," in the divine spirit which inspired Sangster on the upper Saguenay at Trinity Rock, and in the higher reality which Lampman discerned when he communed with his "clearer self" – or even his frogs. Religious idealism surely characterizes E. J. Pratt's Christ-like truant, A. J. M. Smith's neo-metaphysical God, and Hugh MacLennan's vital life-force, imminent in both man and the natural world. It is a mountain-top vision of innocence which enables David Canaan to transcend death in Buckler's *The Mountain and the Valley*, and utopian dreams are to be found in Canadian poetry from Goldsmith to Cohen. Clearly, there must be something fundamentally wrong with Atwood's reasoning when it is controverted by so much of our literature. Furthermore, it could be plausibly (if pointlessly) argued that Chaucer's Troilus, Shakespeare's King Lear, Milton's Satan, Swift's Gulliver, Wordsworth's Michael, Hardy's Tess and T. S. Eliot's Prufrock are all victims of one kind or another who struggle to survive. It should be obvious that if the victim-survival motif is that common in English literature, it cannot be regarded as the distinguishing characteristic of Canadian.

If the "survival hypothesis" fails to account for certain literary facts and is contradicted by many others, there must be something about the proposition which is inherently incorrect. It is worth noting that the constituent elements of Atwood's theory appear to be a blending of the archetypal criticism of Northrop Frye with the psychological categories of the American sociologist Eric Berne as elaborated in another parlour-game book, *Games People Play*. Specifically, Atwood's five basic victim-positions seem to be adaptations of Berne's game-theory positions but with each Atwoodian position corresponding roughly to one of Frye's archetypal modes. Thus the first three of Atwood's positions can be related to Frye's world of experience, with the irony somewhat accentuated by certain demonic motifs. In this world vision, the typical human being – whether Indian, explorer, settler or immigrant – is a victim, and his deity is an oppressive puritan god. Animals are likewise victims who suffer in fear or panic, and Nature as a whole is depicted as a monster – harsh, cold and lethal. Students of Frye will recognize the picture quickly enough. Atwood's fourth position has to do with life in a world inhabited by creative non-victims, people who live happy natural lives in loving families or as Nature's children. Animals here are centres of irrepressible vitality, and Nature is a living process containing within it the contradictions of life and death. This position corresponds to Frye's archetypal world of innocence. Atwood's undeveloped fifth position, which has to do with mystical insight and visions of paradise where freedom and love prevail, is consistent with Frye's apocalyptic mode.

Although Frye and Berne see the world rather differently, both have formulated static, ahistorical, abstract and one-dimensional categories of understanding, which in Atwood's blending emerge as the Have-Cross-Will-Suffer paradigm – with the cross, of course, made of Atwoodian maple. Both, moreover, have attempted to explain an aspect of reality in isolation from everything else. Berne discusses the psychological "games people play" as individuals and without reference to larger social and historical contexts. Frye seals off the subject of literature by approaching it with a rigorously idealist epistemology and then by postulating the existence of an autonomous literary universe in which art imitates art while providing the imaginative forms which life itself attempts to realize. He further isolates literature from concrete social realities by an Arnoldian attitude towards social class. In Frye's philosophy, literature, as a part of culture, tends to do away with classes by embracing only what is best in each of them. Culture thus provides individuals with a means of transcending social class through individual enlightenment, and through this enlightened individualism societies may avoid what both Arnold and Frye describe as the "anarchy" of class conflict. Frye likewise minimizes the significance of the national characteristics of literatures with his cosmopolitan, anti-internationalist argument that nations themselves are either physical inconveniences dividing men artificially or, at best, territorial environments supplying poetic minds with particular images for the autonomous universe of the imagination. Despite Atwood's professed concern for the victims of exploitation and her strong nationalist sentiments, she manages to modify only slightly Frye's idealist liberal and cosmopolitan understanding of the social genesis of literature. Specifically, one finds in Atwood the epistemologically idealist argument that "patterns of theme, image and attitude hold our literature together" and that these patterns are a reflection of a "national habit of mind." This "national habit of mind," however, is to be understood by a reading of Canadian literature, whose patterns can provide lost individuals with a geography of the intellect. Atwood's logic runs within a closed circle of mental forms with only occasional cryptic allusions to non-mental factors which might have something to do with the alleged existence of a victim mentality in Canada. Atwood's liberalism makes her even less aware than Frye of the way in which economic and social relations within Canada have shaped modes of understanding, even among artists. Canada "as a whole," she suggests, can be variously regarded as a "victim," "an oppressed minority," and a "collective victim." Thus no significant distinctions are made between oppressors and oppressed with their divergent ways of seeing the world through literature. Her notion that the high road to Canadian liberation is to be found by each individual's discovering a level-5 utopia through imaginative insight is likewise consistent with Frye's Arnoldian ethic.

Atwood's understanding of nationality conforms to her idealist epistemology and utopian individualism. A nation seems to her to consist merely of the people inhabiting a territory and united by a symbol. We are told that "every country or culture has [at its core] a single unifying and informing symbol . . . which holds the country together and helps the people in it to cooperate for common ends." This definition is not unlike the view held by Frye in 1943 when he informed his *Canadian Forum* readers that "there is an attitude of mind distinctly Canadian" and that "poetry is not a citizen of the world: it is conditioned by language and flourishes best within a national unit." How very different is this early Frye-Atwoodian idea of nationality from that which prevailed among literary critics in Canada prior to World War I. Then there was general agreement that a nation consisted not just of a territory and a poetic mind but of a people with a unique history, a unique social fabric, a unique language and unique customs and institutions. It is worth noting, moreover, that Atwood dedicates her book to a group of idealist critics and poets of the archetypal school – Jay MacPherson, D. G. Jones, James Reaney, Eli Mandel, Denis Lee and Northrop Frye – all of whom would agree with Frye that the history of literature is essentially the displacement of myth with regard to plausibility and that it has little to do with the concrete struggles of nations or classes.

Atwood's criticism probably reveals more about the poetic world-vision of Margaret Atwood than about the structural principles of Canadian literature. Her criticism, in fact, is in many ways an extension of her poetry, and the connections are fairly obvious. In "Some Objects of Wood and Stone," the disconsolate poetic speaker is a disaffected, alienated observer of the "wooden" masses, who are deemed to be as static, multiple, uprooted and transplanted as the totem poles in Stanley Park. In *Survival*, Atwood argues that the literature of her community is essentially a tale of alienated victims struggling to survive. In "Some Objects . . ." we are informed that all traditional values are meaningless and dead. In *Survival*, Atwood affirms that most Canadian literature is written in an ironic mode with no worthwhile gods. In "Some Objects . . . ," it is suggested that reality is to be found in a self-enclosed private world, which language can neither break out of nor break into. The argument of *Survival* is that certain "positions" or psychic states are the essence of literature. The lonely speaker in another poem, "The Islands," takes pleasure in the formal qualities of "symmetry" and "proportion." Atwood the critic finds the recurrence of certain literary patterns personally satisfying. In "The Animals in That Country" the poet suggests that civilization can be politely barbaric or primitively brutal. Atwood the critic argues that Canadian literature is inhaabited primarily by victims – tormented Indians, dying explorers, defeated settlers, etc. In the poem "A Night in the Royal Ontario Museum," Atwood envisions the artifacts of history as a vast jumble of incongruities permitting no exit – a labyrinth which is as idiotic and crazed as modern life. In another poem, even the hard-working pioneer is depicted as a pathetic madman for trying to impose his square mental patterns on a curved natural world. Atwood the critic avoids the problem of "historical development" and implies that it can be nothing more then mere chronology because all advances have been superseded, all rebellions have failed and genuine heroes do not exist except as vague impersonal collectivities. In her poetry, Atwood empathizes and identifies with certain personal figures, notably Susanna Moodie, for whom she can feel a certain personal kinship. In her criticism, she explains that this conjuring up of past personalities, which she calls "totemism," is her way of finding meaning in the past. In much of her poetry, Atwood suggests that man lives in ignorance surrounded by an unknown wilderness and is therefore plagued by anxiety, a basic condition of his consciousness. In *Survival*, she insists that man's environment is usually portrayed in Canadian literature as harsh, violent and cold. In her poetry, Atwood indicates that man's mental life becomes understandable only through the irrational language of myth, in which fantasy and reality mingle. Her criticism is essentially a tracing of myth in Canadian literature. Atwood's poetry expresses a spiritual malaise, a bewilderment and a sentimental personalism which is quite typical of the modernist literary intelligentsia in Canada. Her criticism filters Canadian literature through that same psychic state. What may be an adequate basis for her well made but narrow lyrics is a deficient foundation for an illuminating sociological criticism.

References

Atwood, Margaret. *Survival: A Thematic Guide to Canadian Literature.* Toronto: Anansi, 1972.

Berne, Eric. *Games People Play; The Psychology of Human Relationships.* New York: Grove Press, 1964.

Frye, Northrop. *The Bush Garden: Essays on the Canadian Imagination.* Toronto: Anansi, 1971.

Goldmann, Lucien. "The Sociology of Literature: Status and Problems of Method." *International Social Science Journal*, vol. 19, pp. 493-516.

Logan, J. D. and French, Donald. *Highways of Canadian Literature: A Synoptic Introduction to the Literary History of Canada (English) from 1760 to 1924.* Toronto: McClelland and Stewart, 1924.

MacMechan, Archibald. *Head-Waters of Canadian Literature.* Toronto: McClelland and Stewart, 1924.

McGee, W. J. "Review" [of *Wild Animals I Have Known*]. *American Anthropologist*, vol. 1 (1899), pp. 376-77.

Rashley, R. E. *Poetry in Canada: The First Three Steps.* Toronto: Ryerson, 1958.

Thompson Seton, Ernest. *Wild Animals I Have Known.* New York: Charles Scribner's Sons, 1898.

MARXIST LITERARY CRITICISM AND ENGLISH CANADIAN LITERATURE

ROBIN ENDRES

What is Marxist Literary Criticism?

A Marxist approach to literature can be distinguished from other approaches which have predominated in twentieth century criticism, of which the four major ones are: the mythopoeic (Northrop Frye *et al.*), the Freudian (Leslie Fiedler *et al.*), the formalist (Cleanth Brooks *et al.*) and the sociological. Four concepts central to the Marxist approach to literature are: materialism and dialectics – which are methodological; and alienation and class society – which are concerned with the content of literature.

Marxist criticism is materialist. In the most basic sense, this means that the world is acknowledged as an objective reality, whose phenomena are empirically verifiable. It is in contradistinction to idealism, which says that the world is a product of and determined by human consciousness. The idealists claim that men are separated from beasts because they have consciousness, and that change is the consequence of changed consciousness. One system of ideas can replace another through an act of the will.

Marx, however, argues that what separates man from beast is that man produces his means of subsistence, he produces it of necessity, socially, and this social production is what determines consciousness. At any given historical period, consciousness, or the prevailing ideas of the age, will be determined by the material conditions of men. Further, social production implies a division of labour, and when the mode of social production is capitalism, the division of labour is between the manual labour of the working class and the mental labour of the ruling class. It is this very division which allows the idealist philosophers (themselves members of the ruling or middle class) to overlook the material conditions which are the concrete reality of the working class, and thus to maintain that it is only the "change of consciousness" which affects the lives of men.[1]

There are, not surprisingly, analogies to be drawn between some literary critics and the philosophers criticized by Marx. These critics tend to view all literature, or often the body of literature of one nation, as a self-enclosed linguistic or ethical or mythological (or all three) system which exists independently from the material experiences of people. Some variation of a theory of "creative inspiration" – artists are divinely prompted, or inevitable outsiders, or mystical beings, or akin to the insane – is used to explain artistic production. As far as the content of artistic works is concerned, these critics tend to reduce the "meaning" of such works to a finite list of then irreducible truths about humanity. This list may vary, or may be transferred analogically to another list (of myths or complexes, for example), but the goal is always to reiterate "the external verities of the human condition". As one student put it:

> I find on looking back on years of notes from high school and university that all works of literature, if those notes are correct, tell us a rather short list of rather trite things. Man is torn between Good and Evil. Man strives Onward. Man is saved by Love. Man is doomed to Suffering and Death. Man seeks Truth and Freedom. The whole soulless dictionary of barren cliches is part of the degeneration of the so-called Humanities in the capitalist countries. This partly accounts for why so many students are turned off literary studies and why many literature lecturers in the universities wonder just what it is they are doing and what the social relevance of it all is.

Marxist criticism, insofar as it is materialist, will be concerned with two aspects of art. First, it will raise questions about the social production of art, that is, the material conditions of the society and the artist himself. One could list a great number of such questions, and this is a very fruitful area of literary research. A few examples are: what is the role of private patronage and state subsidy in deciding what gets written or painted and who is chosen to create works of art? What is the relation of technological innovations to the production of art?[2] What is the relation of social class to the opportunities for acquiring artistic skills? In Canada, how do such factors as immigration, the metropolis-hinterland problem, changing patterns in the labour force, and the establishment of such institutions as the Canada Council, the National Film Board and the CBC affect artistic production? Secondly, materialist criticism will concern itself with the way in which content reflects prevailing ideas, and how both are determined, however indirectly, by the mode of social production.

A materialist point of view, however, is only the first step which the critic takes towards a Marxist interpretation of literature. Un-prefixed by the adjective "dialectical," it can result in mechanistic patterns of thought. The type of literary criticism which is analagous to mechanical materialism is one which judges literary works on the basis of the class position of the author, and discusses characterization in the novel solely in terms of the various class positions of the characters. In its most extreme form it condemns all of Western literature as "bourgeois", as merely reflecting the ruling ideas of the ruling class. Good or "progressive" literature is that written by a working-class author about working-class characters and problems, to be read by a working-class audience. Fortunately, this nightmare of bad Marxist criticism is not too prevalent. A suggested term for it is "proletarianism."

The common failing of idealist criticism and "proletarianism" is that both are inorganic. They are essentially static views of literature which do not focus on change and development. Change, or motion, is the first premise of dialectical thought, and it is so because implicit in change is the notion of contradiction:

> Motion itself is a contradiction: even simple mechanical change of position can only come about through a body being at one and the same moment of time both in one place and in another place, being in one and the same place and also not in it. And the continuous origination and simultaneous solution of this contradiction is precisely what motion is. (F. Engels, p. 145)

This contradictory motion, the resolution of which generates new contradictions, is the essence of life, what Engels calls "infinite progress." When contradiction ceases, life ends.

The resolution of a contradiction results in qualitative, as opposed to quantitative change. For instance, when heat is applied to water, it becomes increasingly warm, but does not become steam – a qualitatively new form – until it is heated to exactly 212 degrees Fahrenheit. The most important qualitative change in modern history was the transition from a feudalist to a capitalist economy. Capitalism was preceded by a stage Marx called the "primitive accumulation of capital," when aggregate sums of money were amassed, but were just that – sums of money and not capital.

> He takes as an example the case of a labourer in any branch of industry, who works daily eight hours for himself – that is, in producing the value of his wages – and the following four hours for the capitalist, in producing surplus-value, which immediately flows into the pocket of the capitalist. In this case, one would have to have at his disposal a sum of values sufficient to enable one to provide two labourers with raw materials, instruments of labour, and wages, in order to pocket enough surplus-value every day to live on as well as one of his labourers. And as the aim of capitalist production is not mere subsistence but the increase of wealth, our man with his two labourers would still not be a capitalist. Now in order that he may live twice as well as an ordinary labourer, and turn half of the surplus-value produced again into capital, he would have to be able to employ eight labourers, that is, he would have to possess four times the sum of values assumed above. (Engels, p. 150)

Two further dialectical concepts are the "negation of the negation" and "sublation". When a contradiction is resolved, for instance the contradiction between quantities of money and capital, two things happen. The old situation is negated, and new contradictions arise, in this case the contradiction between the working and ruling classes, between labour and capital. When this new contradiction is resolved in socialist revolution, the negation is negated. But in each case, something of the old contradiction is embodied in the new, is carried forward, and this is called sublation.

Finally, a dialectical view of the world sees a multiplicity of forces at work at all times – an infinite number of contradictions and changes all in various stages and all mutually interdependent. Thus, for instance, the resolution of a given contradiction may be hastened or retarded by another.

Hence dialectical criticism of literature would not simply focus on the ways in which artistic works are determined by the mode of social production, but would examine the manifold ways in which the economic base and the ideological superstructure reciprocally influence each other. It is not a chicken-egg question: the starting point will always be the historical, economic and social conditions which give rise to the particular work of art. But the existence of the work itself is real in the material sense, and insofar as it changes or expands man's knowledge of reality, it enables him to change that reality. Material reality and the actions of men are in perpetual tension, and from this tension arise contradictions, the resolution of which engenders new contradictions.

There is also an interdependence, a mutually reciprocal relationship, among artists themselves and among the works that they produce. In creating a new work of art, the artist negates and sublates previously existing works in the same form or genre. Genres themselves – epics, tragedies, novels – reflect contradictions of the real world and in turn engender their own formal contradictions which are sublated when a new form replaces an old. Jan Kott, the Polish Marxist critic, argues in his work on Shakespearian tragedy that the rise of the bourgeoisie in the sixteenth century resulted in a tragic form that was a qualitative departure from the mediaeval "wheel of fortune" view of tragedy, and that Renaissance tragedy is sublated in modern absurdist drama. When *vers libre* negated rhymed poetry, some of the internal rhythmic structures of the older poetry were maintained. Some genre studies, such as Ian Watt's *The Rise of the Novel,* while not avowedly Marxist, nonetheless contain the basis of dialectical criticism.

Dialectical materialism is the methodological tool essential for a Marxist interpretation of literature. Two other Marxist concepts relate to the content of literature in industrial societies. These are alienation and class. The word alienation has become so over-used by sociologists, the media and the "youth culture" as to be rendered almost meaningless. Yet as it was first defined by Marx in *The Economic and Philosophic Manuscripts of 1844,* it had very precise meaning. The primary contradiction of capitalism – that between the forces of production and the relations of production – results in the exploitation of the worker not just materially, but in all aspects of his existence. The worker produces commodities, but he has no control over this production. The object of his labour – the commodity – is thus alien to him. The commodity itself represents the congealed social forces which produced it – the contradiction between the mode of production which is social and the ownership of the means of production which is private. Further, the commodity assumes symbolic as well as actual power, what Marx called commodity-fetishism. And when things take on more significance than people, people become more and more like things.

The alienation of labour is more than this, however. The product is merely the end result of the process of production. The worker is alienated in the very activity of production itself.

> What, then constitutes the alienation of labor? First, the fact that labor is *external* to the worker, i.e., it does not belong to his essential being; that in his work, therefore, he does not affirm himself but denies himself, does not feel content but unhappy, does not develop freely his physical and mental energy but mortifies his body and ruins his mind. The worker therefore only feels himself outside his work, and in his work feels outside himself. He is at home when he is not working, and when he is working he is not at home. His labor is therefore not voluntary, but coerced; it is *forced*

> *labor*. It is therefore not the satisfaction of a need; it is merely a *means* to satisfy needs external to it.

> ...man (the worker) only feels himself freely active in his animal functions – eating, drinking, procreating, or at most in his dwelling and in dressing-up, etc.; and in his human functions he no longer feels himself to be anything but an animal. What is animal becomes human and what is human becomes animal. Certainly eating, drinking, procreating, etc., are also genuinely human functions. But abstractly taken, separated from the sphere of all other human activity and turned into sole and ultimate ends, they are animal functions. (Marx, p. 107)

The role of culture under capitalism is crucial here. Man is distinct from animals, as we have seen, because he produces the means of his subsistence. He also differs because he is capable of transforming nature *aesthetically*, whether this transformation is functional or decorative. In primitive societies, and in craft production in feudalist economies, aesthetic values and utility values were integrally related. The Indian war canoe, the Eskimo hunting spear, and the patchwork quilt were aesthetically beautiful as well as functional objects – the man or woman who made them was not alienated from his labour. As one Marxist critic put it:

> The enjoyment of beauty is a human response to the sensory richness of the external world. Through working with the things of the world, changing them for human use, the human being discovers not only the structure and use of these things but also their sensuous qualities. What he perceives is real, but he has had to develop the power to perceive it, and so the enjoyment of beauty is also the awareness of his own growth as a human being. The world thus "educated" the human being as he works with it. And so to recognize beauty is to respond to nature "humanized". But nature treated as a commodity becomes nature alienated. (Finkelstein, p. 142-3)

Under capitalism, culture and work are separate, divided

from each other. Leisure is a prerequisite for the appreciation and creation of works of art, and thus art by and large becomes the privilege of the middle class. For the worker, culture – human activity at the furthest remove from animal functions – becomes relegated to the sphere of animal functions. Its purpose is that of escapism, a drug to be consumed along with food, liquor and sex, rather than its potential purpose of expanding and changing human awareness of reality and enabling men to act upon the real material world and to change it. It is important to point out that it is not mass production *per se* which causes the division between work and culture. While the age of the patchwork quilt is no longer with us (however prevalent the back-to-the-land and homemade crafts movement appears) the possibilities of twentieth-century technology foricreative production are virtually unfathomable.

The final, and most devastating consequence of the alienation of labour is the effect it has on the relationships between people.

> An immediate consequence of the fact that man is estranged from the product of his labor, from his life activity, from his species being is the *estrangement of man* from *man*. When man confronts himself, he confronts the *other* man. What applies to a man's relation to his work, to the product of his labor and to himself, also holds of a man's relation to the other man, and to the other man's labor and object of labor. (Finkelstein, p. 114)

Alienation, of the individual from himself and from others, is of course a predominant and powerful theme in twentieth-century literature. Often it is seen, by artists and critics alike, as inherent in human nature. A Marxist critic would of course be concerned with this theme, but would ask questions about the material causes of alienation – indeed would attempt to determine why it is perceived as inevitable by the non-Marxist critic. Incidentally, one reason why pre-capitalist literature doesn't "date" is because in some instances it presents us with a picture of what non-alienated life would be like.

The final concept important for a Marxist critic is the question of class. As much of the foregoing has explicitly or implicitly concerned itself with the nature of class society, it can be dealt with quite briefly here. The fact that the existence of different classes is the overwhelming reality of the lives of Canadians is consistently disguised and mystified by the media, the educational system and the government. Yet literature, insofar as it depicts reality, will directly or indirectly expose the existence of classes. This does not mean that the novelists must say, here comes Mr. X, the exploited worker, getting fired by Mr. Y, his capitalist boss. A good novelist will demonstrate the internal contradictions of the character, enabling the reader to draw his own conclusions as to the causes of those contradictions. It is the task of the Marxist critic to demonstrate the connections, implied or not, between the cause and the conflict. This does not mean that the critic should resort to mechanical "proletarianism," tracking down workers and petit-bourgeois shopkeepers behind every tree. But it is important for the critic to discover the ideological world view, the class assumptions, of the artist.

Non-Canadian Marxist Criticism

There is a considerable body of Marxist literary criticism, both theoretical and applied, which does not deal with Canadian literature. It would be impossible here to discuss all these critics, or even all of the major ones, but the field is dominated by the work of two men, Christopher Caudwell and Georg Lukacs, and any account of Marxist criticism would be inadequate without a discussion of their work. I shall, however, limit the discussion to those aspects of their theoretical work which can be applied to Canadian works. Also, I will deal briefly with the concept of latent and manifest content developed by a contemporary American Marxist critic, Fredric Jameson.

Christopher Caudwell analyzes English poetry from the point of view of "the bourgeois illusion of freedom." The replacement of feudalism by capitalism in European countries was at various historical periods greeted with variations of the cry for liberty, equality and fraternity. Capitalism was an advance because in addition to accelerated technological development it did create democratic institutions. However, these benefit only a minority of people; the majority continue to be unfree to the extent that the surplus of their labour is expropriated.[3] The minority bourgeoisie views all society from its own class perspective, and thus believes that everyone has the benefits that it has. Caudwell claims that this freedom is illusory because, as he quotes Engels, "freedom is the recognition of necessity."

> To the bourgeois, freedom is not the consciousness of necessity but the ignorance of it. He stands society on its head. To him the instincts are 'free', and society everywhere puts them in chains. This is the reflection ... of his revolt against feudal restrictions.... The bourgeois is a man who believes in an inborn spontaneity which secures man's free will. He does not see the man is only free in so far as he is conscious of the motive of his actions – as opposed to involuntary actions of a reflex character, like a tic, or imposed actions of a coercive character, like a shove in the back. To be conscious of the motive is to be conscious of the cause, that is of the necessity. But the bourgeois protests against this, because determinism seems to him the antithesis of free will. (Caudwell, p. 64)

The history of modern poetry, that is from the Renaissance to the present, is a record of what he calls "the gradual self-exposure of this illusion." First the illusion is "a triumphant truth (the growth and increasing prosperity of capitalism)"; then it is "a gradually revealed lie (the decline and final crisis of capitalism)," and finally it becomes its "opposite, freedom as the life-won consciousness of social necessity (the proletarian revolution)" (Caudwell, pp. 68-70).

Caudwell's theory of the bourgeois illusion of freedom is of considerable value in analyzing nineteenth-century Canadian poetry. The early Canadian poets were either immigrants from England or artists whose major cultural identification was with Britain. The conquering of the wilderness and the beginnings of capitalist production in Canada enabled these poets to re-establish the initial stage of the bourgeois illusion, although in an altered form. If the tragedies of Shakespeare and Marlowe celebrated the new vision of boundless individualism freed from the bonds of feudalism, the nineteenth-century Canadian poets like their counterparts, the English romantics, romanticized the labourer. However, this Canadian labourer was not so much proof of pantheism and a nostalgic desire for the simple life (of labourers and children as in Wordsworth) as the creator of the future nation. These poets are often denigrated as weakly derivative of the English romantics. However, Oliver Goldsmith, Charles Heavysege, Charles Sangster, Charles Mair and Isabella Crawford are not retreating to nature *from* industrial society but celebrating and heralding the *establishment* of Canadian industrial society. The most obvious example is Oliver Goldsmith's "The Rising Village," written as a response to his uncle's famous anti-industrial poem, "The Deserted Village." The poem begins with the hopes and hardships of the first pioneers:

> What noble courage must their hearts have fired,
> How great the ardour which their souls inspired,
> Who, leaving far behind their native plain,
> Have sought a home beyond the western main;
> And braved the terrors of the stormy seas,
> In search of wealth, of freedom, and of ease!
> Oh! none can tell but they who sadly share
> The bosom's anguish, and its wild despair,
> What dire distress awaits the hardy bands
> That venture first on bleak and desert lands
> How great the pain, the danger, and the toil
> Which mark the first rude culture of the soil.

The second stanza describes the situation fifty years later: nature, in particular the "savage tribes, with terror in their train" has been conquered –

> And now how changed the scene! the first afar
> Have fled to wilds beneath the northern star;
> The last has learned to shun man's dreaded eye,
> And, in his turn, to distant regions fly.
> While the poor peasant, whose laborious care
> Scarce from the soil could wring his scanty fare,

Now in the peaceful arts of culture skilled,
Sees his wide barn with ample treasures filled;
Now finds his dwelling, as the year goes round,
Beyond his hopes, with joy and plenty crowned.

Goldsmith is sublimely indifferent to the fact that the "peaceful arts of culture" he describes and the boundless optimism he conveys as an expression of the establishment of commodity production and cottage industry in Canada are all laid on the foundations of genocide – the slaughter of native people. "The Rising Village" was written just at the point when the Canadian economy was predominantly petit-bourgeois – the artisan and the family farmer – a curious post-feudal, pre-capitalist hiatus. Work was hard, but unalienated; Goldsmith's peasants were small land-owners, not wage slaves. Thus nation-building can still be viewed optimistically – the alienating effects of industrial manufacture are either unforeseen or ignored in Goldsmith's utopian vision:

How sweet it is, at first approach of morn,
Before the silvery dew has left the lawn,
When warring winds are sleeping yet on high,
Or breathe as softly as the bosom's sigh,
To gain some easy hill's ascending height
Where all the landscape brightens with delight.
And boundless prospects stretched on every side
Proclaim the country's industry and pride. (A. J. M. Smith (ed.) pp. 3-4

The Poetry of Isabella Valancy Crawford represents the highest stage – not to mention the best poetry – of this era of pre-confederation poets. In her long narrative poem, "Malcolm's Katie," we find the same optimistic vision of nation-building as in Goldsmith:

Bite deep and wide, O Axe, the tree!
What doth thy bold voice promise me?

I promise thee all joyous things
That furnish forth the lives of kings;

For every silver ringing blow
Cities and palaces shall grow

Bite deep and wide, O Axe, the tree!
Tell wider prophecies to me.

When rust hath gnawed me deep and red
A nation strong shall lift his head.

His crown the very heavens shall smite,
Aeons shall build him in his might.

Bite deep and wide, O Axe, the tree!
Bright Seer, help on they prophecy! (Crawford, p. 215-6)

Freedom is explicitly associated with the ownership of land. Again, we have a vision of individualism based on petit-bourgeois commodity production. Canada offers the immigrant, at this stage of development, the possibility of neither being exploited nor exploiting the labour of others. Max, the hero of the poem, literally hews out a piece of land for himself, winning Katie and defeating, then forgiving, the evil Alfred. Katie's father Malcolm is already a wealthy, established farmer, but one who a generation earlier carried out the hard struggle with the land. Max clearly understands the difference between alienated and unalienated labour when he describes Malcolm's transition from poor immigrant to successful farmer:

He and his brother Rueben, stalwart lads,
Yoked themselves, side by side, to the new plough;
Their weaker father, in the grey of life–
But rather the want age of poverty
than many winters – in large, gnarled hands
The plunging handles held; with mighty strains
They drew the ripping beak through knotted sod,
Thro' tortuous lanes of blackened, smoking stumps,
And past great flaming brush-heaps, sending out
Fierce summers, beating on their swollen brows.
O such a battle! had we heard of serfs
Driven to like hot conflict with the soil,
Armies had marched and navies swiftly sailed
To burst their gyves. But here's the little point –

The polished-diamond pivot on which spins
The wheel of difference – they OWNED the soil,
And fought for love – dear love of wealth and power –
And honest ease and fair esteem of men. (Crawford, p. 195)

Crawford goes farther than Goldsmith in her understanding of the basis of freedom in this early stage of Canadian society; she has Max compare his and Malcolm's means to wealth with those of state, business and church:

. . . Ay, the battle done and won
Means not a throne propped up with bleaching bones,
A country saved with smoking seas of blood,
A flag torn from the foe with wounds and death,
Or Commerce, with her housewife foot upon
Colossal bridge of slaughtered savages,
The Cross laid on her brawny shoulder, and
In one sly, mighty hand her reeking sword,
And in the other all the woven cheats
From her dishonest looms. Nay, none of these.
It means – four walls, perhaps a lowly roof;
Kine in a peaceful posture; modest fields;
A man and woman standing hand in hand
In hale old age, who, looking o'er the land,
Say "Thank the Lord, it all is mine and thine!
(Crawford, p. 196)

Yet the very freedom celebrated by the pre-Confederation poets was providing the productive base – established agriculture and increasingly sophisticated techniques of commodity production – for industrialization, for unfreedom for the majority and the illusion of freedom for the bourgeois minority. The second generation of Canadian poets – Bliss Carman, Archibald Lampman, Charles G. D. Roberts and Duncan Campbell Scott – can be more closely associated with the English Romantics. Their place in the Caudwellian continuum of the bourgeois illusion of freedom is that of seeing man as instinctively free, but bound by the oppressive conditions of industrial society. Thus a sense of personal freedom is found only in an escape from the cities to a wilderness now tamed and solacing rather than threatening. The conquered wilderness is now a refuge from the new threat (the very thing which accounted for the optimism of the earlier poets) namely Change, or more abstractly, Time. The Confederation poets return to tamed nature for nostalgic reasons, to recapture some moment in the past when time stood still and change did not threaten. Either childhood (as in Charles G. D. Roberts) or a lost and mystical lover (as in Bliss Carman) represents pre-industrial peace of mind. These poems are elegaic and sad – the pre-industrial past, recalled in moments of reflection away from the city, is always overshadowed with the knowledge that it is the past, irrevocably lost. In "The Tantramar Revisited", Roberts returns to the scene of his childhood to compare the idyllic surroundings of his past with the ceaseless change of the present:

> Summers and summers have come, and gone with the flight of the swallow;
> Sunshine and thunder have been, storm, and winter, and frost;
> Many and many a sorrow has all but died from remembrance,
> Hands of chance and change have marred, or moulded, or broken,
> Busy with spirit or flesh, all I most have adored;
> Even the bosom of Earth is strewn with heavier shadows, –
> Only in these green hills, aslant to the sea, no change!

Yet only the poem itself retains and expresses the changlessness of the poet's past. After a long description of what things were like *then*, the poet does not complete his journey to the past:

> Yet will I stay my steps and not go down to the marshland, –
> Muse and recall far off, rather remember than see, –
> Lest on too close sight I miss the darling illusion,
> Spy at their task even here the hands of chance and change.[4]

Similarly, Carman's "Low Tide at Grand Pré" is a nostalgic elegy for the past; here a lost lover and the poet's mystical union with her represent the suspension of time and the possibility of staying "the hands of chance and change":

> So all desire and all regret,
> And fear and memory, were naught;
> One to remember or forget
> The keen delight our hands had caught;
> Morrow and yesterday were naught.

The timeless moment, even in memory, cannot be sustained; the low tide is inevitably superseded by the flood:

> The night has fallen, and the tide . . .
> Now and again comes drifting home,
> Across these aching barrens wide,
> A sigh like driven wind or foam:
> In grief the flood is bursting home.

Lampman's poem "The City of the End of Things" is an example of the "self-exposure" of the bourgeois illusion of freedom. When the Confederation poets look to the city, there can be no nostalgia, not even a vanishing memory. Lampman's poem is basically religious, a depiction of hell and a vision of the apocalypse. The description of the city, however, is not of a Sodom and Gomorrah, but of modern industry. The images are not so much of sin, as of the alienation of the assembly line:

> Where no thing rests and no man is,
> And only fire and night hold sway;
>
> Cease not, and change not, night nor day.
> And moving at unheard commands,
> The abysses and vast fires between,
> Flit figures that with clanking hands
> Obey a hideous routine;[6]

Nineteenth-century English Canadian poetry, with some adjustments, can be interpreted according to Caudwell's theory. Useful as "the bourgeois illusion of freedom" is, however, it falls into the all too common trap of Marxist criticism. That is, it is too epochal, too sweeping in its generalizations. As soon as actual poems are looked at, the tool becomes clumsy and awkward. For instance, although the theory of escapism to nature in order to provide the illusion of freedom applies to the Canadian romantic poets, the pre-Confederation poets were not writing about an illusion of freedom, but an actuality. Early Canadian pioneer society did provide an opportunity for unalienated work – not the freeing of the bourgeoisie from feudal bonds, but the "freeing" of the immigrant from wage slavery to the petit-bourgeoisie. At that time, Canada provided the opposite movement from that of Europe. Instead of small independent commodity producers in Europe being proletarianized, some of the unemployed were able, through emigration, to attain or regain petit-bourgeois status. The optimism of the poets of this period is less that of the ruling class on the ascendancy than of the Horatio Alger, hard labour rewarded by success, fable. Furthermore, poems, and the ideology of the poets who write them, are contradictory. Many of our nineteenth-century bourgeois poets were socially conscious, as we saw in some of the passages from Crawford's "Malcolm's Katie". Lampman was a Fabian socialist, a fact seldom taught with his poems in high school English courses; Duncan Campbell Scott wrote with some understanding of the culture of native people (although his activities in the Department of Indian Affairs were not commendable). Finally, both Caudwell and Canadian anthologists overlook the significance of what is mistakenly called the "counter-tradition" of protest poetry. Protest poems are called a "counter-tradition" simply because they are allowed to go out of print, and are poorly or not at all represented in anthologies of Canadian poetry. Because the tradition is excluded by the bourgeois-controlled publishing industry does not mean that so-called backwoods poets like Alexander MacLachlan were not the *major* nineteenth-century poets, that is to say, the most widely read. A poem like Alexander MacLachlan's "We Live in a Rickety House" cannot be said to express any bourgeois illusion of freedom:

We live in a rickety house,
In a dirty dismal street,

Where the naked hide from day,
  And thieves and drunkards meet.

And pious folks with their tracts,
  When our dens they enter in,
They point to our shirtless backs,
  As the fruits of beer and gin.

And they quote us texts to prove
  That our hearts are hard as stone,
And they feed us with the fact
  That the fault is all our own.

It will be long ere the poor
  Will learn their grog to shun
While it's raiment, food and fire,
  And religion all in one.

I wonder some pious folks
Can look us straight in the face,
For our ignorance and crime
  Are the Church's shame and disgrace.

We live in a rickety house,
  In a dirty dismal street,
Where the naked hide from day,
  And thieves and drunkards meet.[7]

Apart from Margaret Fairley's articles in *New Frontiers*, a radical cultural journal published in the 1850's, and her anthology *The Spirit of Canadian Democracy*,[8] nineteenth-century protest poetry remains uncollected, hidden away in archives and rare book rooms.

When we turn to twentieth-century poetry, the Caudwell thesis becomes more problematic. First, bourgeois ideology is not monolithic. Our contemporary poets represent multifarious world views; if the majority of them can be said to be bourgeois, it is still necessary to delineate carefully just which aspect of bourgeois thought is being expressed, and whether, in some cases, bourgeois concepts are being attacked. Are they being attacked for the right or the wrong reasons? The *oeuvre* of any given poet may pass through various stages. Sometimes an individual poem can convey contradictory ideas, or its ideas may contradict its emotional impact. Second, although Canada is a developed capitalist nation, it has its unique bourgeois traditions and culture. Indeed, in recent times the most important factor in Canadian poetry has been the struggle in itself has its progressive and retrogressive elements. In applying Caudwell to modern poetry, the literary critic must guard against mechanically imposing the views of a critic of English literature on Canadian literature, while at the same time avoiding the parochial pitfall of rejecting the theory simply because it comes from a foreign source.

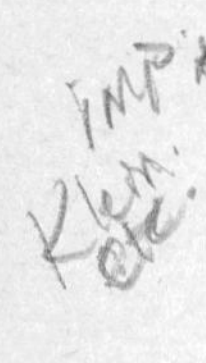

In very broad and general outlines, then, Caudwell's application of the bourgeois illusion of freedom to twentieth-century poetry applies to Canadian poetry. As the illusion becomes harder and harder to maintain, the poet retreats increasingly into a private world. The function of poetry becomes less social and more directed to an elite coterie of readers. The romantic illusion of escape in nature persists but in most cases escapism too becomes private and increasingly self-destructive. Nostalgic memories of childhood and lost love are substituted with escapism into insanity and even death. Poets like A. J. M. Smith who cling most tenaciously to the bourgeois illusion of freedom, who imitate T. S. Eliot and admire the metaphysical poets for the wrong reasons, sometimes see the only freedom in their own death. Smith actually wrote a poem called "My Death", the last two stanzas of which are:

It lies dormant at first –
Lazy, a little romantic
In childhood, later a thirst
For what is no longer exotic.
It lives on its own phlegm,
And grows stronger as I grow stronger,
As a flower grows with its stem.

I am the food of its hunger.
It enlivens my darkness,

Progressively illuminating
What I know for the first time, yes,
Is what I've been always wanting.[9]

Caudwell is also right in pointing out that many poets generalize the competitive laws of the capitalist market into inevitable laws of nature. Anne Wilkinson's "Nature Be Damned" begins:

Pray where would lamb and lion be
  If they lay down in amity?
  Could lamb then nibble living grass?
  Lamb and lion both must starve;
  For none may live if all do love.[10]

Less overt examples of the natural inevitability of competition, poverty, exploitation and struggle – which are really the result of capitalist economic relations – abound in modern Canadian poetry. One example is, "The Lilac Poem", by Raymond Souster, who writes poems which "sympathize" with the downtrodden but at the same time capitulate to the sad inevitability of their "lost" state.

Before the lilacs are over and they are only
shrunken stalks at the ends of drooping branches,
I want to write a poem about them and their beauty
brief and star-shining as a young girl's promise.

Because there is so much made of strength and wealth and
  power,
because the little things are lost in this world,
I write this poem about lilacs knowing that both
are this day's only: tomorrow they will lie forgotten.[11]

At first glance, those who do not possess "strength and wealth and power" are being commended by Souster because he is writing a poem about them. However, just as it is *inevitable* that lilacs are short-lived, so these unsung masses also *naturally* fade away unnoticed. The tone of the poem also contradicts Souster's verbal intention. He attempts to make the reader feel sad about all things of fleeting life and promise – lilacs, young girls and the poor and weak. Then the reader is to feel grateful to Souster: after all, – *he sees* the little sparrows.

As the poet's role becomes increasingly less social, and indeed increasingly less relevant to capitalist society, he may retreat into art for art's sake, or over-exaggerate and inflate the role of his own poetry, even if no one is listening. According to Caudwell, the poet

> begins to set craft skill in *opposition* to social function, "art" in opposition to "life." The craftsman's particular version of commodity-fetishism is skill-fetishism. Skill now seems an objective thing, opposed to social value. The art work therefore becomes valued in and for itself. (Caudwell, p. 24)

Modern Canadian poetry seems, by and large, to have avoided the surrealist and dadaist schools of the 1920's. Our skill-fetishists are more contemporary, and derive their techniques not from France but from fashionable contemporary American styles. Poets like Victor Coleman and b p nichol are skill-fetishists who describe their work as "breaking through the barriers of linear language" and themselves as "conceptual artists." In fact they celebrate incomprehensibility to an ever narrowing circle of friends. On the other hand we have poets who make exaggerated claims for the role of poetry in Canadian society. Al Purdy's "Lament for the Dorsets" is such a poem, that is, an aesthetic manifesto.[12] The extinct Dorsets are compared to twentieth-century society – the Dorsets, like us, were unaware of their immanent extinction as a race. However, an ivory carving, like Purdy's poem, is left behind, implying that cultural artifacts are the true records of lost civilizations. The assumptions – that our civilization is dying, and that Purdy's poems (or poetry in general) will survive, are presumptuous and self-aggrandizing. The real cause of the poet's pessimism is the fact that in capitalist societies poets are essentially ignored and expendable. The possibility of forming a society where this would not be the case is not considered. The bourgeois illusion is again escapist – some future society will know us through Purdy's poem, as he knows the Dorsets through an ivory carving – thus the poet escapes the doom awaiting the rest of us.

Dorothy Livesay is one of the few twentieth-century Canadian poets who has neither fetishized craftsmanship nor restricted her poetic statements to aesthetic manifestoes. With increasing skill and sophistication she has rejected the bourgeois illusion of freedom in favour of the Engelsian version – freedom as the consciousness of necessity. The transition in her poetry from early imagist poems to socialist realism to documentary poems indicates a struggle to convey socialist ideas poetically – that is, both ideologically and structurally. For example, an early socialist realist poem, "In Green Solariums" discusses the transition from the bourgeois ideas of freedom to Marxist ideas of freedom in terms of a *story*. A young girl does housework for a wealthy family, becomes pregnant by their son, is thrown out, and goes to work as a waitress in downtown Toronto. There she learns the lesson "That one lone rebel does no good at all," and eventually commits herself to revolutionary activism. The poem ends with a vision of the proletarian uprising:

> Yet it will come! I watch the city sleep
> And wake each morning with a wider look,
> A restlessness of movement, a hoarse shout,
> That sometimes hurls defiance down a street.
> The time will come. Snow will be shaken off,
> Stripped from the trees by struggling fists and arms –
> Snow will be trampled in the streets, and more!
> Snow will be bloody in the alley-ways.
> We will march up past green solariums
> With no more fear, with no more words of scorn:
> Our silence and the onrush of our feet
> Will shout for us: the International's born! (Livesay, pp.72-5)

In many ways this is a naive poem, not so much in terms of its message, as in its relative lack of attention to structure. In rejecting "art for art's sake" of some of the earlier poems, the poet has sacrificed form for content. In the later political poems, major advances in wedding structure to meaning were achieved (major not just for Canadian poetry, but for all lyrical political poetry). In "Day and Night" (Livesay, pp. 120-5), a basic Marxist concept is conveyed by the use of metre, by sound as well as sense. The concept is that the proletariat, by virtue of the mode of production which is social, already has the basis for organizing to seize the means of production which are privately owned. This is what is meant by the phrase in the Communist Manifesto, "capitalism is its own gravedigger," for by constantly revolutionizing its base, by increasing the socialization of production, capitalism provides the basis for its own destruction. "Day and Night" is a narrative poem which alternates stanzas of long and short lines. The short-line stanzas at the beginning of the poem are meant to convey rhythmically the experience of the assembly line – short, mechanical movements of men made into machines:

One step forward
Two steps back
Shove the lever,
Push it back

While Arnot whirls
A roundabout
And Geoghan shuffles
Bolts about.

One step forward
Hear it crack
Smashing rhythm –
Two steps back

Your heart-beat pounds
Against your throat
The roaring voices
Drown your shout

Across the way
A writhing whack
Sets you spinning
Two steps back –

One step forward
Two steps back.

Here the terse two-beat lines and the frequent rhymes seem confining and oppressive. As the men decide to strike, and then to go further and take power themselves, the same metric structure becomes a liberating force – the restrictions of the assembly line become the collective condition through which the individual achieves freedom:

One step forward
Two steps back
Will soon be over:
Hear it crack!

The wheels may whirr
A roundabout
And neighbour's shuffle
Drown your shout

The wheel must limp
Till it hangs still
And crumpled men
Pour down the hill.

Day and night
Night and day
Till life is turned
The other way!

In other poems, such as Souster's "The Lilac Poem", we saw how conditions of capitalism such as poverty are projected onto all of nature as an inevitable and timeless law. In some of Livesay's poems, such as "In Green Solariums" and "Night and Day", the opposite point is made. In transforming productive relations, men will also transform nature – "Snow will be shaken off" and night will become day. When freedom is seen as the consciousness of necessity, man is not the victim of imagined and hostile natural laws (such as Anne Wilkinson's "For none may live if all do love") but the transformer of nature.

Caudwell focussed his theoretical work on poetry.[13] For a Marxist discussion of the novel, we must look to the Hungarian critic Georg Lukacs. Lukacs has written thirty books and fifty essays and articles on the subject of Marxist aesthetics, only a handful of which have been translated. It is more productive, I think, to discuss in depth one chapter in the history of his work than to attempt a superficial survey of all that is available in English.

I have chosen Lukacs' essay "The Ideology of Modernism"[14] for detailed examination because it is a succinct presentation of his views on the differences between modernism and realism. Its theses lend themselves well to a comparative study of some modern Canadian novels, in the light of which we can then try to re-examine his theory. The first distinction Lukacs makes between realism and modernism is the way each trend deals with the problem of alienation, or "solitariness." All literature, whatever its content or form, asks the question: What is man? Man, according to Aristotle, is *zoön politikon* and therefore men, according to Lukacs, "cannot be distinguished from their social and historical environment. Their human significance, their specific individuality cannot be separated from the context in which they were created".[15] Thus the depiction of alienation in the novel must be the result of the social context of the person who is suffering, and this is the case in the novel of realism. The modernist, however, sees this solitariness as an inevitable aspect of human nature, often *the* inevitable aspect of human nature. This constitutes a negation of history, a negation which takes two forms:

> First the hero is strictly confined within the limits of his own experience. There is not for him – and apparently not for his creator – any pre-existent reality beyond his own self, acting upon him or being acted upon him. Secondly, the hero himself is without personal history. He is 'thrown-into-the-world': meaninglessly, unfathomably. He does not develop through contact with the world; he neither forms nor is formed by it. The only 'development' in this literature is the gradual revelation of the human condition. Man is now what he has always been and always will be. The narrator, the examining subject, is in motion; the examined reality is static.[16]

Lukacs points out that no novelist can ignore social background altogether, but for the modernist, it is just that – "the locus they lovingly depict is little more than a backcloth; it is not basic of their artistic intention."[17]

Another difference between the two forms is the way in which they view the concepts of abstract and concrete potentiality. Abstract, or imagined potentialities are greater than concrete ones, but only choice, which leads to action, will reveal which are concrete and which are potential.

> The literature of realism, aiming at a truthful reflection of reality, must demonstrate both the concrete and abstract potentialities of human beings in extreme situations. . . . Abstract potentiality belongs wholly to the realm of subjectivity; whereas concrete potentiality is concerned with the dialectic between the individual's subjectivity and objective reality.[18]

The modernist does not distinguish between abstract and concrete potentiality since he denies (overtly or otherwise) the existence of objective reality. This leads to what Lukacs calls "the attenuation of reality" and the "dissolution of personality," since a world view which sees reality as impoverished will also tend to depict an impoverished subjective world.

The third and for our purposes most important concept is the obsession of the modernist with psychopathology. Morbidity, neurosis, insanity – Marxist and realist novelist alike see these psychological states either as a protest against the prosaic quality of life under capitalism or as a tragic consequence of the frequently unbearable nature of unresolvable contradictions. The debilitating monotony of most jobs, the "forced leisure" of unemployment, the widespread sexual dysfunctions, the discord between men and women resulting in large degree from the unequal position of women in society – surely the list is long enough to condemn the capitalist system and to account for the waiting lists at every psychiatric ward in the country. Yet the modernist fetishizes neurosis – like solitariness, it is an inevitable result of the "human condition."

> Life under capitalism is, often rightly, presented as a distortion (a petrifaction or paralysis) of the human substance. But to present psychopathology as a way of escape from this distortion is itself a distortion. We are invited to measure one type of distortion against another and arrive, necessarily, at universal distortion. There is no principle to set against the general pattern, no standard by which the petty-bourgeois and the pathological can be seen in their social context. And these tendencies, far from being relativized with time, become ever more absolute. Distortion becomes the normal condition of human existence; the proper study, the formative principle, of art and literature.[19]

Neurosis, and its extreme manifestation, insanity or psychosis, is not only inevitable for some modernist writers – it becomes a goal, a *desirable* state of mind. While we might not be quite as harsh as Lukacs in the disparagement of modernism, we would, I think, agree that the fetishization of madness in some modern novels (and on the part of many lay and professional psychologists of the R. D. Laing school) is a variety of anti-humanism which he is quite right to condemn.

One further theory remains to be discussed before examing Canadian criticism, and that is a rather useful critical tool described by Fredric Jameson in his book *Marxism and Form.* It is not the task of the critic, according to Jameson, to *relate* the kind of antitheses I have been mentioning – between the individual and society, form and content, economics and consciousness – because

> ...they always are related, both in our own life experience and in any genuine work of art. Rather, such criticism is called upon to articulate the work and its content in such a way that this relationship stands revealed, and is once more visible. (Jameson, p. 406-7)

One way of revealing these relationships is through the critical technique of inner form, or latent content. For Jameson, the work of art itself is a kind of censorship which mystifies those aspects of the experience of capitalism which are disguised by the bourgeoisie in one way or another. The process of work and the class structure are two examples, although the list could be lengthened considerably.

> ... the terminology of work satisfaction is useful because ... it makes us understand why such an impulse had to be disguised in order to come to artistic satisfaction in the first place. For, particularly in middle-class society, the fact of work and of production – the very key to genuine historical thinking – is also a secret as carefully concealed as anything else in our culture. This is indeed the very meaning of the commodity as a form, to obliterate the signs of work on the product in order to make it easier for us to forget the class structure which is its organizational framework. It would indeed be surprising if such an occultation of work did not leave its mark upon artistic production as well, both in the form and in the content ... (Jameson, pp. 407-8)

Latent content is distinct from "manifest content," the latter being the "themes" and "plot" of a novel. In modern works of literature one facet of latent content is not only production but literary production. Thus for Jameson, the "deepest subject" of Hemingway's novels "is simply the writing of a certain type of sentence, the practice of a determinate style" (Jameson, p. 407). This Heminwayesque obsession with technique, however, is not merely a formal question. The theory of latent content permits Jameson to demonstrate that it is integrally bound up with the idea (in this case a fantasy) of non-alienated work:

> ... the experience of sentence-production is the form taken in Hemingway's world by non-alienated work. Writing, now conceived as a *skill*, is then assimilated to the other skills of hunting and bullfighting, of fishing and warfare, which project a total image of man's active and all-absorbing technical participation in the outside world.... The Hemingway cult of *machismo* glorifies leisure; it reconciles the deepest and most life-giving impulses toward wholeness with a status quo in which only sports allow you to feel alive and undamaged. (Jameson, p. 412)

Inner form or latent content is "both disguise and revelation of the concrete and one of the tasks of a Marxist critic is the reconstruction of this latent content in a particular literary work or genre. Such a line of analysis has particular applicability to a study of Canadian literature and will be discussed in the final section of this article.[20]

Marxist and Historical Criticism in Canadian Letters

Within the confines of Canadian literary criticism there is little explicitly Marxist theory and analysis of works of Canadian literature, at least in academic journals.[21] We can, however, look to some examples of criticism in this country which take as their starting point the historical and social context of literature. In her article "Canadian Tradition and Canadian Literature", Miriam Waddington distinguishes two major trends in Canadian criticism, the "apocalyptic-mythic" and the "historical-social."

> The [historical-social] view has never been more completely articulated than by Archibald MacMechan in *Headwaters of Canadian Literature* (1924), and the [apocalyptic-mythic] found one of its earliest champions in Lionel Stevenson's *Appraisals of Canadian Literature* (1926). . . . The chief exponents of the apocalyptic critical position are Northrop Frye, Roy Daniells, Malcolm Ross, and James Reaney. Somewhere in between the two positions, but closer to the apocalyptic one, is Milton Wilson. A. J. M. Smith seems hard to place because his method is historical; but his attitudes are Christian-mythic, so on the whole he belongs with the apocalyptic group. On the historical-social side we have, in the wake of MacMechan, such figures as E. K. Brown, John Sutherland, Carl Klinck, Frank W. Watt, John P. Mathews, Desmond Pacey, and A. M. Klein. (Waddington, p. 129)

Waddington deals with four issues in Canadian letters – geographic location, colonial origins, bilingualism and multi-culturalism and the "soberness or the northness of the national character" to demonstrate the different ways they are treated by each school. This discussion leads her to the conclusion that the apocalyptic school is explicitly or implicitly reactionary in its ideological outlook:

> Still less effective as agents of social change are aesthetic values and manifestos. Aesthetic categories are always theoretical, and a difference of opinion in that sphere remains abstract and does not change the course of national affairs. And it is a well-known fact that aesthetic categories blend more easily with mythopoeic interpretations of literature than do historical or political ones. There is therefore less risk of change, and less necessity for political action in adopting the apocalyptic approach to Canadian tradition, rather than the historic one. (Waddington, p. 137)

Implicit here too is an explanation of the relative popularity of the mythopoeic school.

The historical approach is not without a great deal of merit for the Marxist critic, and although space precludes a survey of all the articles and prefaces written in this vein, a consideration of two important works is warranted. In his Preface to an anthology called *Other Canadians*, John Sutherland makes two seminal points for Canadian criticism. Attacking A. J. M. Smith's preference for "cosmopolitan" rather than "native" Canadian poetry, Sutherland proceeds to counter the general tendency on the part of Canadian critics to insist on the separation between poetry and reality:

> It it time we began stating . . . that the poet retains human attributes in spite of being a poet, that his materials are tangible often in spite of appearance, and that he has something to say which frequently has meaning for the ordinary man. We accept the value of this idea where prose is concerned, and often judge it with regard to its relevancc to reality. Why then, do we regard poetry in a totally different way? May it not be that the actual environment is even more essential in the case of poetry? Does not the poet work upon

> everyday things so as to extract their essence and give it back to us in a more concentrated, meaningful form? Does he not, therefore, have more to tell us about common ideas and feelings than the prose writer possibly can? (Dudek and Gnarowski, pp. 55-6)

This may seem a commonplace idea to most of us now, but at the time (1947) it represented an important departure in Canadian criticism.

At various times throughout the history of literature in this country writers and critics have bemoaned the lack of, or cried for the need of, literature which deals with specifically Canadian themes and subjects. Sutherland, however, was one of the first literary critics to make the connection between a socialist view of the world and Canadian content. Poetry which uses Canadian themes statically – empty symbols of nationalism such as the flag or the maple leaf – in reality glorifies the British empire and is thus colonialized, self-apologetic poetry. On the other hand, poetry which takes a socialist stance but which imitates the left-wing writers of England is equally colonial. As Sutherland says:

> One reads a poem which purports to be written from the socialist point of view, and is reminded more of the work of Lewis Carroll than of Karl Marx. The air of make-believe is due partly to the face that the middle-class Marxist poet comes from England into an environment doubly alien because it is passing through a period of special change. (Dudek and Gnarowski, pp. 57-8)

For Sutherland, the establishment of socialism in Canada is contingent upon the breaking of colonial ties, and therefore the task of Canadian writers is to develop a poetry which is also free of the dependence on forms prevalent in the imperialist countries:

> Socialism must take a somewhat different form in every country, and in Canada it cannot be separated from a healthy national point of view. We cannot proceed to the

setting up of a socialist society before we greatly weaken or break our colonial ties, which in the economic sense are important and in the spiritual sense are well-nigh crippling. ... Just at the time when socialism has become the most important national issue, one would expect to find poets who would express the aims of the people, and to see a new life and freedom enter into Canadian poetry as a whole. But such freedom exists only in the limited sense described above, and our literary colonialism tends to be heightened by this political development. (Dudek and Gnarowski, p. 58)

Sutherland, like some of his successors, notably Milton Acorn, tends to over-emphasize colonialism at the expense of considerations of class structure *within* Canadian society (as well as the extent to which Canada is itself an imperialist power), yet his analysis is central to any Marxist discussion of the role of nationalism in Canadian literature.

Margaret Atwood's *Survival: A Thematic Guide to Canadian Literature* which is being widely used in high school and university curricula, seems at first view difficult to classify.[22] This is because Atwood tries to get the best of both worlds – while solidly rooted in the "apocalyptic-mythic" school (she is a former student of Northrop Frye) the book purports to be a political study as well. On the one hand, it analyzes individual works formalistically – in terms of a self-enclosed system of myths and images; on the other it sees the central them of *all* Canadian literature – namely that of the victim – arising from the cultural domination of Canadian letters by Britain and the United States. For the Marxist, politics cannot be divorced from history, and the "thematic" approach is by definition ahistorical. Atwood's political position, on the surface fashionably radical, is bourgeois individualism. Her solution to cultural oppression is not collective struggle, but "the creative non-victim position." This is "consciousness" politics, "changing one's head" through an act of the will. Those unable to achieve the creative non-victim position are relegated to the hopeless ranks of victim positions one through three. As in the works of the poets praised in *Survival* – bill bissett and Dennis Lee – social reality is either ignored or seen as a wilderness to be kept outside the private world of the non-victim's "head." Unfortunately, the attacks from leftist social scientists on "victimology" – identifying the victim in order to blame him – have not found their counterpart among cultural critics.

Equally pernicious is Atwood's literary analysis. It is not only Atwood's over-emphasis on negative symbols in Canadian literature (which critics of all political persuasions have found fault with), but also basic assumptions about the process of literary creation are incorrect. Many of the examples of "negative symbols" ("Given a choice of the negative or positive aspects of any symbol – sea as life-giving Mother, sea as what your ship goes down in; tree as symbol of growth, tree as what falls on your head – Canadians show a marked preference for the negative")[23] are based on the supposition that artists consciously choose symbols which are then intended to refer back to real experience. In fact, the opposite tendency – describing objective situations which then become generalized through their symbolic heightening – is both an explanation and a description of the literary process in the majority of Canadian novels. In other words, "negativism" is more often a marked tendency towards realism – the actual and particular exigencies of the struggle with nature in Canadian society – than symbolic nihilism or self-immolation on the part of the guilty victims of colonization. The struggle itself is dialectical – one step forward, two steps back. Whether a character or group of characters in a novel is successful or not, the *struggle* for integration with nature (that is, of the individual and society) is in itself a positive phenomenon. Any mechanical separation of exploiter/victim, positive/negative, pessimistic/optimistic ignores literature which is or tries to be genuinely dialectical.

Finally, just as Atwood ignores the dialectical relationship between characters and environment in novels, she ignores the relationship between the work of art and the receiving public. To do so completely misses the ironic effect which many Canadian novels and poems have on their readers, whether or not the author intends it. Thus the reader's response when struggle fails may not be despair but determination to overcome similar obstacles, or to look for other solutions. The reading, as well as the writing of literature, is a social act.

The Theories Applied: The Novel

It now remains to attempt a practical application to Canadian fiction of some of the theories I have been discussing. To do this fully, examining all the prose written in Canada, is of course out of the question; to do it only partially runs the risk of distortion, that is, hunting for examples which will fit theories, rather than proceeding from induction. For the most part then, I will suggest problems and areas of research, but will discuss in detail two novels in terms of Lukacs' comparison of realism and modernism, and one novel in terms of Jameson's theory of inner form.

Margaret Laurence's *The Stone Angel* and Margaret Atwood's *Surfacing* are similar novels in many ways. The central character of each is a woman out of touch with the people in her world, both unable to feel or express feelings of affection for those she loves, and unable to recognize their feelings for her. Both novels are first-person narratives, and the problems and advantages of this form as it relates to the theme of alienation are similar. Both Hagar Shipley and the unnamed heroine of *Surfacing* learn to overcome their isolation and the plots of both novels revolve around this final resolution. Both novels are more symbolic, more modern than the novels of classical realism, and both are less modern or symbolic than the classical modern novel such as Kafka's *The Trial.* Yet placed on a Lukacsian continuum between realism and modernism, *The Stone Angel* is a realistic novel and *Surfacing* is a modern novel, and herein lies the clue to the very different ways in which each novelist deals with the same social and artistic problem.

The first-person narrative form is effective to the extent to which is successfully conveys irony, that is, the extent to which it allows the reader to see things about the character which the character does not see about herself. Irony is resolved at the moment or moments when the character does see those things. This is another way of saying that the form is successful insofar as it reveals the inner contradictions of character and the causes of those contradictions. Critical judgement is implied here, for if those all-important casual connections are not made through ironic devices, the inner contradictions will either appear as inevitable and therefore irresolvable, or, what is more likely the case, we will be confronted with what Lukacs calls the "disintegration of personality." In *The Stone Angel*, irony is achieved through the device of extensive flashbacks in Hagar Shipley's memory, so extensive in fact that we have a double narrative – two stories told about the same woman by the same woman. The paradoxical situation which Laurence manipulates so brilliantly is that clarity is revealed through the confusion of Hagar's mind. She is confused in the sense of being senile, but more importantly confused in the sense that she does not understand the significance of her memories at the time at which they happened, and as they relate to what is going on in the present. Yet because we have two time periods to compare, we come to an increasing understanding of her character, since we see a causal connection between events in her past, and the situations she is mystified by in the present. By the use of a contemporary form – we might say a *filmic* device – Laurence permeates her novel with historicity. The relationship between alienation and social background which Lukacs cites as the main virtue of the novel of realism is revealed in *The Stone Angel* through the double narrative.

Another consequence of this device is that although Hagar misjudges and misinterprets the actions of others, we perceive that they too are suffering from the same sense of isolation. This is especially clear during the passages when she is reliving the relationship with her brothers and her sons. She does have some understanding of the ways in which her father was unable to love her, but very little of the ways in which she in turn is unable to love her brothers, husband and sons. Yet because she responds to them in the same way that her father responded to her (although she doesn't realize this), we understand that the isolation is reciprocally imposed: that each character is hurting and hurt. Even though we only see the present-day Marvin through Hagar's distorted vision, we know that he is more than the methodical, uninteresting paint seller that she shows us because we know that she has done to him what her father has done to her and her brothers.

The main difficulty with the first-person narrative form is the danger of depicting characters other than the main one solely through the voice of the narrator. If the narrator's problem is the fact that her emotional life is atrophied to the extent that she does not experience feeling at all, as is the case in *Surfacing*, how can we tell if her projection of her friends as also being emotionally sterile is accurate? In the first part of the novel there is some doubt in our minds – Joe does not seem merely malicious, and some sympathy is evoked for the cruel treatment Anna receives from her chauvinist husband David. The controlling metaphor here is Americanization. The characters in *Surfacing* are not alienated as a result of the ways in which they have internalized the contradictions of life in present-day Canadian society, but because they have somehow allowed themselves to be victims of the creeping Dutch elm disease spreading up from south of the border. Both David and Anna succumb totally by the end of the novel, becoming, though not Americans, like Americans:

> It doesn't matter what country they're from, my head said, they're still Americans, they're what's in store for us, what we are turning into. They spread themselves like a virus, they get into the brain and take over the cells and the cells change from inside and the ones that have the disease can't tell the difference.[24]

They are the machine people, all plastic and metal. Some little hope is held out for the furry-backed Joe, who appears not to be a machine because he is like an animal. Now, not all Americans are machines, and although we have all met people with some of the characteristics of a David or an Anna, people who are not flesh and blood do not exist. Science fiction is a legitimate form but not when it is disguised as something else, in this case a novel. Furthermore, by the end of the book, we are not asked to question the distorting lens of the narrator, but to accept as valid her final and total dismissal of her friends, and as *Atwood's* judgement of them as well. They are literally cardboard characters, and if we accept Engels' "contradiction is the essence of all living things", they are dead characters because they experience no contradictions. The theme of alienation is given an extra twist here – not only is their isolation inevitable, *it is their own fault*. The narrator, however, mysteriously part of a self-appointed elect, overcomes her isolation through an act of the will. And this act of the will is to go insane. "From any rational point of view I am absurd; but there are no longer any rational points of view."[25]

For the last twenty or so pages of the novel, we watch the narrator undergo and recover from a period of five days of insanity. It is a process of purification, in which all the symbols and images scattered throughout the book are fitted into their places in the Atwoodian jigsaw puzzle. Water and land, animal and machine, American and human, mother and father – all the dualities are brought together and tied up into the symbol of the "blood egg," the foetus the narrator has conceived. The experience of insanity is thus more a literary technique than a real, felt human experience. There are some powerful moments in these passages, but they are a result of Atwood's very competent use of concrete language, evident also in her poetry. But her considerable power in this regard is at odds with a world-view that is rather frightening in its coldness. The narrator's ability to go crazy is seen as a *virtue*, an experience which makes her morally superior to everyone else in the book:

> But I bring with me from the distant past five nights ago the time-traveller, the primeval one who will have to learn. . . . No god and perhaps not real, even that is uncertain; I can't know yet, it's too early. But I assume it: if I die, it dies, if I starve it starves with me. *It might be the first one, the first true human*; it must be born, allowed.[26] (Italics mine)

Surfacing exhibits the three major philosophical short-comings which Lukacs saw in the modern novel. First, the social milieu is only a backdrop; although Atwood describes in some detail the northern Ontario bi-cultural locale, the details remain unassimilated and unrelated to the processes undergone by the characters. To quote Lukacs again. "The narrator, the examining subject, is in motion; the examined reality is static." In the case of *Surfacing*, "the examined reality" also includes the other characters. Second, the question of abstract and concrete potentiality is slightly more difficult because of the ending of the novel. Since objective reality is only a backdrop, potentiality in the novel is abstract, rather than concrete. Yet the narrator does make a choice at the end of the novel – the choice to give birth, a concrete potentiality certain to become an actuality. Yet the queen bee narrator seems to have conceived this child also through parthenogenesis. Like the nervous breakdown, it is a literary symbol. Finally, the reification of insanity supports Lukacs' chain reaction: abstract potentiality leads to dissolution of personality leads to flight into psychopathology.

Laurence, too, uses literary techniques to bring Hagar Shipley to an understanding of the causes of her isolation – the classical Christian symbol of the descent to the underworld. Here, however, the descent myth is used to deepen and enrich the actual experience of the character, and this experience is above all a *social* one. Hagar runs away from Marvin and Doris' house and takes a bus up the coast of British Columbia. She makes her way down a steep cliff and spends two days in a deserted house in what was once a fishing village. During this time we learn, through her memories, the story of her son John's death. She is joined by an insurance salesman who apparently comes to this place often for his secret drinking. She is as bored by him as no doubt others are by her, until he relates the story of his own son's dying in a fire while he is at a prayer meeting. At this point Hagar has one of her rare moments of contact with another person:

> He thinks he's discovered pain, like a new drug. I could tell him a thing or two. But when I try to think what it is I'd impart, it's gone, it's only been wind that swelled me for an instant with my accumulated wisdom and burst like a belch. I can tell him nothing. I can think of only one thing to say with any meaning.
>
> "I had a son," I say, "and lost him."
>
> "Well," he says abruptly, "then you know."
>
> We sit quietly in this place, empty except for ourselves, and listen for the terrible laughter of God.[27]

Her sympathy is repaid, when, upon wakening, she mistakes in a senile moment the insurance salesman for her son John, and asks his forgiveness. At the beginning of the book, Hagar had been unable to impersonate her dead mother by putting on the latter's shawl for her dying brother Dan. Now, the salesman pretends for her that he is John:

> "I didn't really mean it, about not bringing her here. A person speaks in haste. I've always had a temper. I wouldn't want you to feel you always had to be going out somewhere. . . ."
>
> I've spoken so calmly, so reasonably. He can't in all conscience refuse what I've said. I wait. At last I hear his voice. An inexplicable sound, a grating, like a groan or a sob. I grow anxious, and think he may still be angry. But when he speaks, his voice is not angry at all.
>
> "It's okay," he says. "I knew all the time you never meant it. Everything is all right. You try to sleep. Everything's quite okay."
>
> I sigh, content. He pulls the blanket up around me. I could even beg God's pardon this moment, for thinking ill of Him some time or other.[28]

Hagar's descent has not been from the world to the underworld, but from a Calvinist world view (truth is truth) to a more understanding and forgiving humanity, which recognizes that sometimes we must lie to one another when the truth is too painful. The beginning of Hagar's recognition of this has come about through human involvement, made more meaningful through the use of a Christian mythological framework and the various images and thematic patterns brought to bear on this scene.

Neither of these novels ignores social and political background – if anything, *Surfacing* is more explicit in its concern with political issues, especially the American domination of Canada. In *The Stone Angel*, however, the social background is in fact not a background; the milieu of the characters is integrally bound up with their aspirations, decisions and shortcomings. Furthermore, Laurence achieves this on a metaphorical level, through the central image of the stone angel. The novel begins:

> Above the town, on the hill brow, the stone angel used to stand. I wonder if she stands there yet, in memory of her

> who relinquished her feeble ghost as I gained my stubborn one, my mother's angel that my father bought in pride to mark her bones and proclaim his dynasty, as he fancied, forever and a day.

Jason Currie, the stern, Scotch Calvinist merchant, is the richest man in Manawaka, and grills his children with the family motto and various sayings to the effect that he is a self-made man. Later Hagar puts her own children through the "gainsay who dare!" chant. His sin, and hers, is pride, obtained at the suppression of tolerant and compassionate instincts represented by the dead mother, and symbolized by the stone angel. Currie is not an unfeeling man (as his remarks on the death of Lottie Dreiser's mother indicate); the point is that in order to be successful in the new world it was necessary to be stern and proud. Yet pride manifested in Hagar is her curse, and she is humiliated when she tells the wealthy Lottie Dreiser that she has been working as a domestic. Pride is thus a Christian sin as well as a human failing arising from and related to specific economic and social conditions. Similarly, Mathew's bitterness and John's self-destructiveness are partly of their financial inability to obtain an education. The tension between potentiality and the thwarting of that potentiality for all the characters is what gives the novel its tragic and its hopeful tone. Laurence, as Marx said of history, begins with the living, thinking, feeling human being.

The social background in *Surfacing* is an external menace called Americanization. It literally attacks from the outside and turns organic flesh into inorganic material. There is no sense of people struggling with themselves, their world, their friends and lovers. Thus the political part of the novel is merely timely, and the overall effect is to provide readers with a sense that they are participating in a topical issue. Similarly, we are presented with a slick picture of the alienation of four young, educated Canadians, without ever being required to confront our own isolation. The past of the heroine is presented as a series of artifacts which she burns or slashes during the period of insanity – it is never lived through. Returning to Lukacs, we would have to decide if the reason one novel succeeds and the other fails is a technical reason, based on his distinction between realism and modernism. I tend to criticize *Surfacing* not because of its modernism (indeed, its strongest points are its very contemporary linguistic merits) but because it is less humanist than *The Stone Angel.* Laurence has increased our tolerance through her literary art – we understand Hagar better than if we had met this old woman in the flesh. As Hagar herself comes to realize in her encounter with the insurance salesman, human beings are more than the sun of their parts, however superficially boring or unattractive those parts may be.

Turning to Jameson and latent content, I will just briefly mention some novels which I think lend themselves to this kind of analysis before discussing Sinclair Ross's *As for Me and My House* as one representative example. There are a number of novels which centre on the working-class family, urban or rural. This is of course obvious in such novels as *Cabbagetown* and *The Tin Flute*, whose authors are aware of the class restrictions of their characters; that is, manifest and latent content coincide. But what about a novel like *The Mountain and the Valley*, where an analysis of latent content would link David's inability to become an artist (the manifest content) with his desire to "forge the uncreated consciousness of the race" which is being economically forced into extinction? A discussion of Buckler's use of tree imagery alone would indicate an interesting progression from the Christmas tree, central metaphor for the family, at the beginning of the novel, through to the acres of stumps David sees when he finally climbs the mountain at the end, thus laying bare the latent content of regional depression. Martha Ostenso's *Wild Geese* and the novels of Laura Goodman Salverson, not to mention Marie Claire Blais and her Québécois successors, arc further examples. Interesting, too, that three of the most successful plays in the current renaissance of Canadian theatre – *Wedding in White, Leaving Home* and *Forever Yours, Marie Lou* – are all more or less realistic dramas about working-class families. We might also look at such class factors as the proletarianization of characters like Hagar Shipley and Philip Bentley as they affect the shape of the novels in which they appear.

Two inescapable facts of Canadian social life are regional disparity and the presence of ethnic minorities. The regional novel is certainly predominant in Canadian fiction, and the effects of regional underdevelopment and cultural differences could be traced through dozens of novelists from Ethel Wilson in British Columbia to Percy Janes in Newfoundland. The oppression – latent or manifest – of ethnic groups, could be examined in Austin Clarke, Abraham Klein, Adele Weisman, Mordecai Richler, Gabrielle Roy's *Windflower*, Laura Salverson and so on. Finally, the role of women in Canadian society could be dealt with not just in terms of the content of our fiction, but also in terms of the relatively large number of women writers who have contributed to the Canadian novel. And, following Jameson's study of Hemingway, could we comment on the style of our female writers as it relates to inner form? It is my view that the presentation of women characters in Canadian novels by men is qualitatively different from other novels in English, Leonard Cohen notwithstanding. Although there are unfortunate elements of the Henry Miller, D. H. Lawrence, Norman Mailer "holy virgin/dirty slut" syndrome in the Canadian novel, for the most part our male authors create women who are more than symbols of male sexual fantasies – world-historical people in their own right. MacLennan's Peggy Wain is a ship designer; Austin Clarke's *The Meeting Point* is about a West Indian domestic who works for a wealthy family in Forest Hills; Grove's women are intelligent central characters. Even Morley Callaghan, from whose Catholicism one would expect variations on the two Marys, gives us Anna in *They Shall Inherit the Earth* – a young girl in danger of becoming a prostitute not because of sin or temptation but because she is so poor she is almost starving. And then, of course, there is Mrs. Bentley in *As for Me and My House*.

As for Me and My House is ostensibly a frustrated-artist novel about Philip Bentley, a not-so-young minister in a small prairie town during the depression. Philip is hopelessly trapped. The illegitimate son of a waitress, he enters the ministry in order to get an education he would not otherwise be able to afford. Thus the premise of his faith is a hyprocritical one, which results in a great deal of bitterness and self-contempt. Furthermore, he is saddled with a wife to support at a time when churches were unable to pay their ministers. His double burden makes him doubly frustrated. He has given up painting except for cruelly sardonic portrayals of the false fronts of the town of Horizon. The Bentley marriage is childless, another cause of Philip's resentment, and he lavishes attention on Steve, an adolescent orphan boy who comes to live with them. Sinclair Ross, to my knowledge, has made no statements about his intentions in this novel, but the preceding description would seem to approximate the character he was trying to depict. However, he has used a rather unique stylistic device – the entire novel consists of excerpts from Mrs. Bentley's diary. Thus one component of its inner form is the story of Mrs. Bentley, the story of the Canadian wife. Everything that happens to Philip happens to Mrs. Bentley in spades. She is punished for being an economic and emotional burden, and punished for not providing another burden – a child. The fact that she too is approaching middle-age and must do without most necessities and the smallest luxuries must be borne with womanly and Christian cheer. Her life consists of small and large sacrifices. Indeed, she seems hardly aware of the greatest sacrifice, giving up a career as a concert musician in order to marry Philip. The one talent which initially attracts him is the talent she must renounce in order to keep him. This is the nexus of female oppression in marriage, at least for the woman who works or wants to work – the damned if you do, damned if you don't syndrome. This tension characterizes Mrs. Bentley's life and gives the novel its frequent insights into the psychology of oppression or what is often called the colonized mind:

> ...I must still keep on reaching out, trying to possess him, trying to make myself matter. I must, for I've left myself nothing else. I haven't been like him. I've reserved no retreat, no world of my own. I've whittled myself hollow that I might enclose and hold him, and when he shakes me off I'm just a shell.[29]

The novel is also a study of what the contemporary women's movement has called "tension-management" – that marital phenomenon where husband and wife are aware of the wife's superior abilities in some matters. The wife tries to disguise these abilities for the sake of the male ego, but the disguising itself is resented. This dynamic is illustrated on the first page and continues throughout:

> It's been a hard day on him, putting up stovepipes and opening crates, for the fourth time getting our old linoleum down. He hasn't the hands for it. I could use the pliers and hammer twice as well myself, with none of his mutterings or smashed up fingers either, but in the parsonage, on calling days, it simply isn't done....
>
> He looks old and worn-out tonight; and as I stood over him a little while ago his face brought home to me how he shrinks from another town, how tired he is, and heartsick of it all. I ran my fingers through his hair, then stooped and kissed him. Lightly, for that is of all things what I mustn't do, let him ever suspect me of being sorry. He's a very adult, self-sufficient man, who can't bear to be fussed or worried over; and sometimes, broodless old woman that I am, I get impatient being just his wife, and start in trying to mother him too.[30]

As for Me and My House is more a symptomatology of a marriage than a novel. The operant symbiosis is that the love-starved wife craves affection to affirm her reality as a person and a woman, and the husband can only dispense tenderness and affection at the expense of his own manliness (as he perceives manliness). Although the false fronts in Horizon are blown down in the life-giving rainstorm, Mrs. Bentley does not essentially change – she merely increases her sacrifices (adopting Philip's illegitimate child without letting him know she knows it is his child) in order to facilitate change in *his* life. If he is able to work as an artist, then she will be the recipient of some of the emotional spin-off. Beyond the interlocking, internecine struggles of the Bently marriage is the larger structure of work and its meaning, the real inner form of the novel. In twentieth-century Canadian capitalist society,... the only classes able to achieve a limited form of non-alienated labour are the petit-bourgeois and the professional.[31] The real nodal point of the despair experienced by both Mr. and Mrs. Bentley is their inability to use their respective work skills. Philip is a victim of the economic disaster of the depression, complicated by his hypocrisy and his painful awareness of that hypocrisy. Mr.s Bentley is oppressed by poverty but also is thwarted by societal and marital chauvinism. Because, as professionals, their potential could have been realized, Ross shows us that the human need, the need for self-fulfilment through labour, is frustrated.

Conclusion

There are two basic problems facing the Marxist critic of Canadian literature. First, Marxist aesthetics in general is the most underdeveloped branch of Marxist theory, with the possible exception of Marxist psychology. The concepts developed by Caudwell and Lukacs are, in my opinion, of great value; yet they suffer from over-generalization, a contradiction between the theory and its applicability to specific texts. Second, no systematic examination of Canadian literature from a Marxist point of view – any Marxist point of view – exists. How can we lay the groundwork for such studies? The theories discussed here (as well as other models which I have omitted, such as structuralism and semiotic theory) can and should be refined and adapted to indigenous literary problems. However, just as it is the task of any literary critic to constantly refer back to the literary text, it is the task of any Marxist critic to constantly refer back to the basic theory of Marxism. Marxist *methodology* must be applied to Canadian literature in the latter's historical and social contexts.

The precision with which dialectical materialism can be used as a tool for understanding literature depends on the degree of particularity of examples used. This is one reason why genre distinctions are of importance to Marxist critics – poetry, novels and plays all arise from different social conditions. Although from a contemporary point of view their distinctions may not seem important they do fulfil qualitatively different social functions. Likewise, distinctions must be made within genres, between "myth" novels and novels of realism, between lyric and narrative poems and so on.

Good literature elicits feelings and ideas. In poetry, this is achieved through various ways of patterning words; in the novel through the description of the feelings of characters; in the drama, through action. All three are created and received in specific cultural contexts such that the feelings and ideas of both writer and reader are constantly shaped and re-shaped. The Marxist critic has the task of analyzing this process and delineating its contradictory aspects with as much precision as possible. This task is didactic: its purpose is to help the Canadian reading public develop critical standards so that they in turn will demand literature which serves their aesthetic and social needs.

Notes

1. See F. Engels and K. Marx, *The German Ideology* (Moscow: Progress Publishers, 1968).

2. Harold Innis has laid the groundwork for this type of research in Canada. See especially, "The Strategy of Culture," in *Contexts of Canadian Criticism*, Toronto: ed. Eli Mandel (University of Toronto Press, 1971).

3. The men and women who became workers gained and lost under capitalism. Gained because as labourers and no longer peasants or craftsmen they constitute the social base of production and therefore the potential to revolutionize production; lost because of poor working conditions, economic privation and the alienation discussed above.

4. *The Oxford Book of Canadian Verse* (Toronto: Oxford University Press, 1960), pp. 66 and 68.

5. *Ibid.*, p. 86.

6. *Ibid.*, p. 79.

7. *Ibid.*, p. 12.

8. Progress Books, Toronto, n.d. Now out of print.

9. *Op. Cit.*, p. 214.

10. The Oxford Book of Canadian Verse, p. 283.

11. Gary Giddes and Phyllis Bruce, *ed. Fifteen Canadian Poets* (Toronto: Oxford University Press, 1970), p. 65.

12. *Ibid.*, pp. 36-8.

13. However, Caudwell's *Studies and Further Studies in a Dying Culture* (New York: Monthly Review Press, 1971) includes chapters on George Bernard Shaw, D. H. Lawrence and H. G. Wells.

14. G. Lukacs, *Realism in Our Time: Literature and the Class Struggle* (New York: Harper and Row, 1971).

15. *Ibid.*, p. 192.

16. *Ibid.*, p. 21.

17. *Ibid.*, p. 21.

18. *Ibid.*, pp. 23-4.

19. *Ibid.*, p. 33.

20. The reader may have noticed that the pagination of the above quotations is in the 400's, and 400 pages is about as long as it takes Jameson to get to the point. Jameson is the guru of the current spate of Marxist literary criticism in the U.S. academies, and a through-going critique of his work is essential. Although he claims to be a Marxist, one has the disturbing intuition that in a crunch he would change the sign in front of his bus to "Hegel" and drive off in the other direction. At one point he actually slaps his wrists for the unpardonable sin of using examples to illustrate his points:

> For it is clear that up to this point our description has been essentially undialectical to the degree to which it has taken dialectical thought as its *object* only, and has failed to underscore its own self-consciousness as thought to the second power. That this is the case may be judged from the dominant category of the present essay, which is that of the *example*: for only where thought is imperfectly realized is it necessary to offer examples as such. (p. 338).

Self-criticism is an admirable trait, but not when one's all too occasional Strengths are seen as the only weaknesses. Jameson's prose style is astonishingly turgid, and the use of such words as "re-abolish" and "occultation" is a little frightening in the work of someone concerned with aesthetics. Reading *Marxism* and *Form* is like listening to someone who has returned from a prolonged visit in a foreign country and who seems to have forgotten how to use his own native language. An article in *College English*, Vol. 34, No. 2, November 1972, entitled "The Great American Hunter, or, Ideological Content in the Novel," is a decided advance.

21. There is, of course, a body of work to be found in the nineteenth-century labour periodicals and in the left-wing press of the twentieth century such as *Masses, New Frontiers, Canadian Mercury, Western Clarion* and some issues of the *Canadian Forum*. See also V. I. Hanes, "Northrop Frye and Marxism," in Horizons, *The Marxist Quarterly*, No. 24, Winter 1968 and Milton Acorn, "On Not Being Banned by the Nazis," in *More Poems for People* (Toronto: New Canada Press, 1972).

22. Margaret Atwood, *Survival: A Thematic Guide to English Canadian Literature* (House of Anansi Press, 1972).

23. *Ibid.*, p. 35.

24. Margaret Atwood, *Surfacing* (Toronto: McClelland and Stewart Ltd., 1972), p. 129.

25. *Ibid.*, p. 159.

26. *Ibid.*, p. 191.

27. Margaret Laurence, *The Stone Angel*, New Canadian Library No. 59, (Toronto: McClelland and Stewart Ltd., 1964), pp. 233-4.

28. *Ibid.*, p. 247-8.

29. *Sinclair Ross, As For Me and My House*, New Canadian Library No. 4 (Toronto: McClelland and Stewart Ltd., 1957), p. 75.

30. *Ibid.*, pp. 1-2.

31. Professionals are petit-bourgeois insofar as they produce their own commodities – a painting or a Ph.D. thesis – over whose distribution in the market they have some control. They do not create surplus value. The current capitalist crisis sees increasing numbers of professionals, such as engineers, who are either unemployed or selling their labour power to large corporations. Compare this to the self-employment or the relative freedom of the academy.

References

Caudwell, Christopher. *Illusion and Reality.* New York: International Publishers, 1937. P. 64.

Crawford, Isabella Valancy. *Collected Poems.* Toronto: University of Toronto Press, 1972. Pp. 215-6.

Dudek, Louis and Gnarowski, Michael. *eds., The Making of Modern Poetry in Canada.* Toronto: Ryerson Press, 1967. Pp. 55-6.

Engels, F. *Anti-Duhring.* Moscow: Progress Publishers. 1969. P. 145.

Finkelstein, Sidney. *Existentialism and Alienation in American Literature.* New York: International Publishers, 1965. Pp. 142-3.

Fredric Jameson, *Marxism and Form: Twentieth Century Dialectical Theories of Literature.* Princeton, New Jersey: Princeton University Press. 1971. Pp. 406-7.

Livesay, Dorothy. *Collected Poems: The Two Seasons.* Toronto: McGraw-Hill Ryerson, 1972. Pp. 72-5.

Marx, Karl, *Economic and Philosophic Manuscripts of 1844.* New York: International Publishers, 1964. P. 107.

Smith, A. J. M. *ed., The Oxford Book of Canadian Verse.* Toronto: Oxford University Press, 1960. Pp. 3-4.

Waddington, Miriam. "Canadian Tradition and Canadian Literature," *Journal of Commonwealth Literature.* December 1969. P. 129.

PART 2: DEVELOPING A NEW CONTEXT FOR CRITICISM

INTRODUCTION
PAUL CAPPON

When James Steele shows the roots of Atwood's "survival hypothesis" in older idealist traditions of Canadian literary criticism, and when these traditions are related to liberal ideology, we have already an idea of the directions which must be taken in the development of a new, context for criticism and of an activist sociology of literature. With Endres' essay, we can trace through her textual analysis the traditions of Canadian literature and criticism back to their ideological foundations; so that we already begin to identify literature whose social content and whose forms and aesthetic values combine to produce progressive writing.

The analyses of Steele and Endres thus represent a point of departure for a new context for criticism upon which the essays of of Part Two build. This new context for criticism must take account of the second problem which we stated in the introductory essay to be crucial to developing a sociology of Canadian literature: the problem of patronage and publishing. John Fraser's essay on "The Production of Literature" deals with that problem in its relationship to the situation of the Canadian writer and of the kind of literature which is produced as a result of a specific system of production.

Fraser situates the problem of production of Canadian literature in a context which is partially shared by all countries of the capitalist world. That context is the transition from "enterprise" to monopoly capitalism, eventually with increasing State intervention in the attempt to smooth over irrationalities of the system. During this transition, culture is transformed from one participation and activity to one of consumption of leisure. We have seen that the growing surplus, requiring the expansion of the markets of the cultural industry even across national borders, necessitates the growth of consumerism (passive consumption) in every branch of economic and social activity. When literature is viewed as a process not only of writing but of reading, this transition to passive consumerism has profound social impact. Already the literary product had been commodified – produced for a market mechanism over which the writer had no control, so that he is alienated by his labour which is appropriated by others. Now under the monopoly capitalist phase the tastes of the public are easily manipulable, and this in turn reflects back on the kind of literature which is produced.

The phenomenon of transition to the monopoly capitalism phase and its cultural impact is common to the capitalist world, but its specific character in Canada takes the unique form discussed by Fraser. This form has two elements of great importance. The first relates to the penetration of American capital investment in the Canadian cultural industry described in the introductory essay. That American dominance gave rise in the 1960's to a resurgence of a type of Canadian nationalism. But Fraser shows that the attempt to establish a national market (Canadiana) did not necessarily lead to political unity and Canadian autonomy. Still less did it lead Canadian writers to an understanding of their own situation or that of the class system within Canada. This fact leads Fraser to an important analysis of the historical situation in which the Canadian writer has been placed by the economic and social evolution of the country as it affects cultural production. Examination of the historical situation of the Canadian writer helps to explain the ideological impasse of authors, believing, as Fraser says, "neither in socialism or capitalism." Under such conditions of ideological confusion among artists and writers faced with the current system of production and distribution of cultural artifacts and ideas, an activist literature would seem difficult to develop.

Robin Mathews' "Developing a Language of Struggle in Canadian Literature and Literary Criticism" is in some respects a summary of what we have learned about our literature and of what we now must do with it. To develop a language of struggle in literature against imperialism and against current class structures, Matthews would not do away with all past literature and literary criticism which is not part of the new activist context for literary criticism. But he expects us to learn from them: "Literature provides an exploratory tension between what has been, what is, and what should be."

Mathews echoes the theme of the introductory essay in insisting that the first prerequisite of a progressive literature, of the development of a language of struggle is that writers have at all times a structural understanding of Canadian society and of its historical context. This structure and historical context constitute for Mathews the unique identity (termed in the General Introduction above the concrete material roots) from which the author must write. In desiring the writer to have an historical materialist understanding of Canadian society, Mathews regards the liberal position as reflected in our literature as one of "false consciousness' – the failure to perceive social reality in its totality, especially the contradictions of the class system. This failure to have a class analysis denies in writers the creation of a "literature which deals with the possible." Like structural-functionalist sociology to which it is ideologically akin, such failure supports the status quo and impedes social change.

If Mathews' development of a language of struggle begins with the kind of class analysis which the introduction has outlined, using it to deal with past literature – as Endres, Steele and Aspinall have done – it must also incorporate the recognition that those who are not part of the directing class do possess the strength and potential to change the social order. Mathews then goes beyond Endres' opposition of realism to modernism by positing a Canadian *socialist* realist literature as an element of the class struggle and of anti-colonialism. The example of the author's choice of an entrepreneur as protagonist in the *Master of the Mill* provides for Mathews, a context for the struggle for social change as workers are chosen as protagonists by Canadian writers.

Mathews therefore conceives of the development of a language of struggle as one involving class analysis; an understanding by the writer of his situation and the historical context of the country; the use of a realist mode which eventually may be prefixed by the word "socialist" when it deals with structural problems from the viewpoint of workers, not only from that of bourgeois or of the alienated middle class; the presentation of Canadians of all classes with human understanding notwithstanding their class role. Finally, Mathews deals also with the question of the relationship between aesthetics and progressive social content. A progressive writer cannot be self-satisfied on account of the social content alone of his writing. One thinks immediately of the idealized "proletarian" writing which Endres condemns or of what often passes for socialist realism in Eastern European states, particularly the Soviet Union – glorification of the rule of a technocratic-bureaucratic dominant class. This kind of writing is usually stagnating in petrified forms which might at some time and place have had real meaning as revolutionary literature, but which, when stylized and copied as support for a heavy-handed status quo, turn into the opposite. Mathews therefore implies that socialist realism and the development of a language of struggle in the Canadian context will have as much to do with language, form, and aesthetics as with the actual content, for these are all bound together in literary work. This suggests to him that progressive literature in Canada may be called upon to create its own modes. Using our understanding and critique of past literature and literary critique, developing an historical materialist sociological analysis of Canada, integrating language, progressive form, social criticism and content – these seem to be the steps toward a progressive Canadian literature and the goal of the engaged sociology of Canadian literature.

DEVELOPING A LANGUAGE OF STRUGGLE: CANADIAN LITERATURE AND LITERARY CRITICISM

ROBIN MATHEWS

A re-examination of the sociology of English Canadian literature in the terms of its anti-colonial possibilities and with regard to the development of a language of struggle brings us to questions which are half-hidden from view because the ruling ideology is actively against the creation of an anti-colonial movement in Canada. The questions can only be articulated and answered as history moves, for the milieu must shift. Paradoxically, the milieu will shift as a very function of the questions being asked and being accepted as serious questions. That last statement implies bringing into consciousness the real terms of our social being which will be, in itself, a force for change.

At the present time we may not speak, in any serious way, about "the ideas Canadians have" or "the Canadian sense of our condition." We speak of the present state of consciousness in Canada. We seek to understand what Canadians know about the country and what they want for its future. We must realize, however, that the Canadian people are conditioned by the class in power to express ideas that may be actively harmful to the future and wellbeing of the country. The social structures are not currently available, and a state of consciousness does not exist in which Canadians think freely and knowingly about the state of Canadian society. If they did, they would recognize – both as critics and as imaginative writers – the existence possibilities for anti-colonial action that could emerge from consensus based upon a common awareness of class, capitalism and colonialism. Literature, wouldn't necessarily become "thesis" literature in such a situation. It would not necessarily become, that is, literature which points to an obvious political moral. But it would be clear about the effects upon plot, character, structure and aesthetics that result from class, capitalism, colonialism and the historical struggle of the people to secure a just community. Literature would locate itself at a new level of class awareness. Instead of relating to traditional middle-class protagonists or with individualist heroes who reject and "leave" society, the people of Canada would ask for heroic values expressed in different terms.

The critics of literature wouldn't demand "thesis" or propaganda literature. When the centre of works of literature moved from courtly figures and aristocrats to middle-class figures, the literature was not propaganda literature. A shift in class focus in literature simply mirrors a recognition in general consciousness that a new class has gained legitimacy. Critics, then, would point very clearly to class bias in writers, to blindnesses of writers to dominant class psychology prepared and superimposed upon writers and, to some degree, upon readers of literary work in Canada. They would call for and eventually help produce, for example, a novel about an active unionist which would convey the heroism and humanity of the protagonist and the dehumanizing effects and manipulation of capitalism. A "Philip Grove" would arise, and instead of writing a great novel about a family of entrepreneurs, a ruling class family, such as the Clark family of *Master of the Mill*, he would write a great novel about the family and life of Bruce Rogers, the union organizer, a man for whom Grove had great sympathy but saw as a pawn in the ineluctable movement of capitalism to its imperial and neo-colonial phase.

When we say that Canadians exist in a bourgeois capitalist society, economically and culturally dependent and exploited in classically colonial terms; that our only institutionalized political movement not frankly capitalist is inexhaustibly and characteristically social democratic; and that we suffer particular and unique problems, we begin to see the kind of soil out of which our literature comes, the milieu to which our writers give voice. When we list some of our particular problems and unique conditions, we begin to comprehend that our total identity is unique and demands a unique balancing of the contradictions of place, people and history.

To begin, Canada has had an almost unbroken colonial history divided among three major imperial powers. Secondly, Canada has major territorial proximity to the most powerful imperial state ever recorded in history, a state which has significant, escalating control over the life and economy of this country. Thirdly, Canada has vast raw materials used for false barter in order to maintain a significant store of widely accessible luxury goods and an illusion of independent national wealth. Fourthly, English Canada has worker organizations effectively framed, fragmented, and controlled from the imperial state. Fifthly, English Canada, especially, shares a common continental language which makes easy and invisible the direction of ideas and culture in Canada from the U.S.A. Sixthly, the territorial area known as Canada houses two major cultures the roots of which are significantly different and the languages of which are different. Knowledge of each culture in the other culture is almost nonexistent. Both cultures know much more about U.S. imperial culture than they know about each other. Finally, Canada is currently pervaded by a liberal ideology which unflaggingly supports colonialism and dependency in Canada. It is an ideology which ultimately affects even the finest liberation movements. When we fully understand these things, we see the kind of soil out of which our literature comes, the milieu to which our writers give voice, and the consciousness in which writer, critic, and reader alike, are immersed.

At one level (once again seeking precision about our real condition) we must face the fact that our writers write out of a sensibility heavily afflicted with false consciousness. The phrase "false consciousness" simply means that the person perceives the reality of the social structure as he or she is conditioned to do so by dominant class interests for the benefit of those interests. The person doesn't perceive the reality of social structure as it really is. When we say that our writers work from a sensibility often heavily affected with false consciousness, we must fully understand the writers' condition and we must not romanticize or idealize their role.

Canadian writers, in that respect, are not particularly different from others of their kind elsewhere. The writer is not *generally*, in serious revolutionary terms, one of the "unacknowledged legislators of the world" as the English romantic poet, Percy Bysshe Shelley, would have us believe. The writer quite conventionally conveys and communicates "intelligence," already analysed and organized on behalf of the dominant class and, therefore, on behalf of the dominant explanations of reality in the society. He/she usually only extends consciousness about the developing, shifting, and extending accents and emphases of the prevailing (and, therefore, ruling) philosophy, or ideology, or accepted set of principles in the society.

In brief, for example, materialist, capitalist, individualist society has moved increasingly towards exploitation in erotic, sensationalist terms. It has done so because the person of the individual becomes sacred and increasingly the focus of reality as historical, group, and class values are denied as existing. Intense exploitation of the body as erotic object is possible in a society that separates, individualizes, and alienates people from one another. The exploitation is, of course, commercially profitable at a hundred levels. The undefended individual, fragmented from the group, is a hundred times more available for persuasion than is the person possessing group values, access to past experience, consciousness of legitimacy in class terms.

Intellectual argument and the forms of imaginative work go parallel with economic, physical and commercial development of conditioned "reality." Writers generally exploit the same values but present them as new, daring revolutionary breakthroughs in consciousness. In fact, the intelligentsia simply legitimizes the whole exploitive process the inherent in the philosophy of the *real* wielders of power in Canadian society. The role of the erotic and sensational experience in daily life is a subject for wide discussion. The modern "liberation" of the subject has been in accord with a capitalist, individualist, exploitative philosophy, the philosophy of greed. George Grant discusses "the capitalist philosophers . . . involved with "the emancipation of greed' " in his essay, "Canadian Fate and

Imperialism."[1] Grant discusses them, of course, from a conservative, Christian point of view. But he puts his finger deftly on the historic move to capitalist, individualist materialism of which modern erotic, sensationalist writing is simply a contemporary manifestation.

Irving Layton, for whom an early Marxist period is claimed, is presented as one of the liberators of sexual and individualistic expression in Canada from puritan (narrowly Christian) and socially conventional forces. In fact, he is, at one important level, an advertising man for the philosophy of greed. So deeply rooted is his mock-liberationist false consciousness that his poem, "For Mao-Tse-Tung: A Meditation of Flies and Kings," suggests that he and Mao-Tse-Tung are alike, brothers of elite sensibility who rise above "the meek-browed and poor/ in their solid tenements," to make a name for themselves. Layton's love poems are usually powerfully chauvinist statements of the male speaker's right to employ the female as a sexual object quite unrelated to anything but an erotic contact.

Writers are not magicians. They are, instead, the conveyors of intelligence – the *intelligentsia.* They are the interpreters, the spokesmen and women of society. It follows that a society possessed of a profoundly false consciousness will produce a majority of writers who are afflicted with false consciousness. Anyone who would use that fact, however, to damn Canadian literature would be a fool, unless at the same time, he or she were to damn nearly all the literature of the West on precisely the same basis. If, however, we are to get to a language of struggle and to genuinely anti-colonial possibilities in our criticism and literature we are going to have to come to terms with the ubiquity of false consciousness in Canada. To realize that Canadians do not see into the real condition of the country is not to grow contemptuous of them. For the colonial condition which invites us to seek anti-colonial possibilities is a condition which, by definition, is cursed with a deep and pervasive condition of false consciousness in the population. Quite apart from its role as a conscious instrument of struggle, literature is a repository of the states of mind that have been manifested in a society. It records the ideas of form, the concepts of order, the modes of determining value, the motives people in a society have had for attempting definitions of beauty. As such, literature permits an understanding of *identity* because it presents the terms of life peculiar to a particular milieu. It provides, moreover, a dialectic among states of identity. The past, the present, and the future are brought together in a tension that permits identity to be seen as continuous without being monolithic or simplistic. Literature provides the possibility of an exploratory tension between what has been, what is and what should be.

The roots of struggle, the bases of necessary change in Canadian society must be found in the reality of Canadian society, not in a fantasy about it or in an inapplicable or irrelevant theory of revolution. That means the real identity of Canadians must be the basis for struggle; the real capabilities and potentialities of Canadians must be liberated. The failures of the Canadian people must be faced squarely, analysed sympathetically and placed in historical context. Seeing our failures, seeing them in terms of the aspirations of Canadians at their best, makes possible a struggle rooted at once in the recognition of error and in the celebration of visible strengths and potentialities. Hugh MacLennan, Margaret Laurence, Adele Wiseman, and Morley Callaghan all, at some point in their work, denigrate or demean the ideas of socialist struggle and socialist society. They all – to put it another way – treat serious Leftist activity in capitalist Canada as a kind of whimsy or aberration. Their reasons for doing so must be fully understood in terms of the failures of the Left as well as the manipulations of the right. We need to know precisely what social forces have acted upon ordinary Canadians, how those forces were effective, and what in the condition of ordinary Canadians led them to accept the negative treatment by MacLennan, Laurence, Wiseman and Callaghan of the ideas and values of the Left. In a very real sense it is not only foolish but it is wrong to blame ordinary Canadians – the Canadian people – for not being conscious of the real condition of the country and their role in its life. For if a dominant class does rule, and if it does control the means of communication, and if it does manipulate the handling of "intelligence," then the ordinary people of Canada have to be lucky, especially heroic, or at least, historically assisted to know their real condition and then how to change it. Our role, as a part of the re-examination of the sociology of

Canadian literature, is to help move Canadians to the necessary point of consciousness.

A study of the sociology of Canadian literature implies a study of the social order and of social history. It means bringing together in mutual illumination real social struggles and the imaginative treatment of those struggles in the literature of the country. From the beginning of Canada an exploiting class contended with the settlers and community builders; the literature mirrors, explores and comments upon the conflict between the two forces. After the conquest of New France, the "two solitudes" fiction of English Canada is almost unwearyingly apologetic for English domination and, later, almost unabashedly federalist in tone and intention. Whatever may be said about English domination – or any domination – federalism is not in itself an evil. But if English Canadians are going to understand what is going on in the "two solitudes" literature in English, in the imaginative writing in Québec which deals with English Canada, and in the day to day relations of "les deux nations" they must read the literature correctly.

By the same token, English Canadian readers must know about the reality of the British and U.S. influences upon the behaviour and imaginations of Canadians. The Canada First Movement, the Imperial Unity Movement and other similar political/cultural expressions very often had a single, simple motivating drive among Canadians. They were motivated by a belief that to become and remain independent, self-respecting and sovereign, Canada has to use Britain to defend itself against the expansionist ambitions of the U.S.A. Canada, they believed, allied with Britain and what have become the Commonwealth nations could hold off the U.S.A., could balance its power. Other forces believed in a primary alliance with the U.S.A., declaring Canada a "North American nation." That phrase simply implies that Canada ought to take its lead from what the U.S.A. declares is relevant to reality.

While there have always been Canadian "independentists," not until recent years has a growing public consciousness emerged which declares that we need not ally with colonizing powers but that we should make our own way as an independent nation. English Canadians must know that the battle raged over the two choice of alliance until the defeat of R. B. Bennett's government in the 1930's, when the MacKenzie King regime then ushered in the full-scale era of Canadian integration into the U.S. empire. The fact of the long conflict is echoed in the literature. The fact of capitulation to the U.S. empire describes the quality of imagination, the forms of expression, the themes developed, and the philosophies which provide the milieus of imaginative works of our time – the works which consent to the fact of our position in the U.S. empire, those which apparently ignore it, and those which fight against it.

Ironically, Canadians were often told that to opt for a British connection was to opt for class oppression, while to opt for a U.S. connection was to opt for an egalitarian distribution of power. Canadians have learned that colonial status in relation to any power means class rule and, moreover, the complex fact of class rule spread confusingly between at least two nations.

The development of Canadian poetry since 1925 but expecially since 1945 connects directly to the increase of U.S. power in Canada and the increasing domination of Canada as a political, economic and cultural dependency of the U.S.A. The influx of U.S. people for whom U.S. poetry and sensibility are central to an understanding of reality is a direct influence of U.S. state power in Canada. Contrary to the mythic explanations of writers unconscious of the milieu in which they live and write, they did not simply reach out for poetic excellence after 1945 and light upon U.S. models. They were the intensely conditioned recipients of imperial expansionist rhetoric and its cultural apologia. A factor in U.S. domination of a significant proportion of Canadian writers at the present time is the effective disabling of those writers in relation to Canadian needs and reality. If they come to believe – as some of them have – that U.S. sensibility defines an active relation to reality, then Canadian sensibility is embarrassing and parochial; and the Canadian tradition is a disappointing provincialism best forgotten and ignored. Just as the managing class in a dependent situation looks to U.S. management skill and to U.S. administrative models, so do poets and other writers look to U.S. leaders in artistic theory and U.S. models of creative excellence. About 1945 John Sutherland, then a leading Canadian critic analysed the influence of the U.S. in Canada – on a rather apolitical and vague-cultural-influences level. He declared that evolution in Canadian poetry would bring Canada heavy U.S. influence and even U.S. schools of poetry in Canada. A scant fifteen years later, at the height of U.S. power and Canadian junior-partnership in the U.S. empire, the Black Mountain poets of the U.S. came to Vancouver, set up a branch plant in British Columbia and have been extending their "school" throughout Canada since. Whether Sutherland was correct in seeing the condition as evolutionary or not, he intuited the relation of political and economic power to art and he prophesied correctly.

A class analysis of the literature of our past doesn't make us reject the literature or hate it. It permits us to see that we have had a major portion of our literature, for instance, which has desired harmonious community with emphasis on a whole people rather than on individualists. That desire is expressed in John Richardson's *Wacousta*, Susanna Moodie's *Roughing It in the Bush*, Sara Jeannette Duncan's *The Imperialist*, Philip Groves' *Fruits of the Earth*, W. O. Mitchell's *Who Has Seen the Wind*, Hugh MacLennan's *Barometer Rising* and *Return of the Sphinx*, Margaret Laurence's *Stone Angel*, Adele Wiseman's *The Sacrifice* and *Crackpot*, to mention only some. The literature reveals, again and again, a desire for viable community based on tolerance and justice, a tendency to meritocracy and egalitarianism, an expression of anti-colonialism. The literature tends to make heroes of the group, the family, or the couple – seen historically, rather than the individual seen anarchistically. Even Haggar Shipley of *Stone Angel* learns that individualism in the end defeats the individual; and in her last days she makes clumsy attempts to express a social identity larger than herself.

A class analysis permits us, moreover, to have a clear view – within the literature and the society – of the real exploiters and exploited. It permits us to see that Canadians as a totality are not guilty of the failures in Canada, but that a specific and definable comprador ruling class in Canada is responsible. That understanding is absolutely essential if we are to make room for struggle and for anti-colonial action in Canada.

A class analysis also reveals, of course, a strong tendency in MacLennan, Laurence, Wiseman, Callaghan, and Richler, as I have said, to reject socialist solutions to national problems. It reveals a tendency to patrician values in Richardson, Duncan, MacLennan, and Susanna Moodie, for instance; and it shows us that writers often suggest the heroism of the educated petite bourgeoisie in a liberal society as the ideal a reader should accept. A class analysis reveals a tendency to idealize order which is under benevolent middle-class direction. A class analysis of the literature of our past permits us to place the values and loyalties of the writers with clarity and assurance.

Our humourists, as I have said elsewhere (Haliburton, Hiebert, Mitchell, Leacock) are all writers closely connected to the dominant values of the day – by class and disposition. But each of them reserves a place for the integrity of the oppressed, and the hero/heroine in their works is often a Canadian man or woman in an oppressed position. Humour in Britain, we know, is often based upon class. In the U.S.A. humour is often based upon the mobility and cunning of a manipulating individualist. In Canada, humour is often based upon the ironic integrity of the oppressed or colonial person or group.

If a class analysis permits us to see our literature of the past clearly, to see – to put the statement another way – the real virtues of our people in clear relation to false consciousness, then a class analysis can work to help create a literature that deals with the possible struggle.

To begin: a class analysis of past literature conducted in full relation to the kinds of problems and characteristics I described earlier as particular and unique must disclose what one might call the movement of Canadian expression through time, the character and identity of the Canadian people. That undertaking ought, as I suggested earlier, to shift the milieu in relation to the questions asked and as a result of their having been asked. What then should result? An ideologically literate corps of writers should result, to begin. If we glance backward at earlier works,[2] we would see that the writers would need to reorganize their materials to reveal the forces of exploitation, of oppression, the forces which connect with the fact that we Canadians exist in a capitalist society in which the dominant class supports our economic, political and cultural dependency.

Those novels don't do that. Rather, they present a view of Canadian society in which the individual is buffeted by personalist forces, usually, which exploit or liberate without the writers' connecting the forces experienced personally to the larger determinants of class and economic power. To say that *does not* mean to say that writers should turn novels into political/economic tracts. It is to say that *the writer* (not the characters in the novel) should be able to place and set actions in such a way that readers understand the relation of particular lives and particular exploitations to the general condition of class, of economic structure, and of historical causes inherent in the milieu of literary "fictions."

Someone said to me recently that it is impossible to make people write in a certain way. The opposite is, in fact, true. It is not only possible to make people write in a certain way, it is inevitable that they are made to do so. The reality of a time – as writers see it – is the reality presented in their literary expression. One need only think of the court poets of the late middle ages to recognize how aware we can be of the limits of the reality of an age dictating the character of literary expression.

We, of course, have our own "court poets," the writers who accept unquestioningly the ruling ideology of the time and engage their literary efforts in a kind of play with the possibilities of that ideology. As a reality becomes conscious in a people and its writers, the desire to articulate that reality *and its implication for character and action* becomes, first, possible and then inevitable. That is no doubt why the play written about the attempt by Canadian authorities to assassinate Tim Buck in Kingston Jail was suppressed very soon after it was written. The implications for character and action among Canadians faced with that expression of the evidence of real class war in Canada – the implications for life and art – could only have threatened the stability of the dominant class. The play was suppressed.

Literature, then, is very often a record of the present state of ruling-class imagination. But it can have a significant role to play in developing a language of struggle. Literary criticism must deal with false consciousness fully and fairly. Writers must risk ruling-class disapproval by making their works comprehensible analyses of the structures of ruling-class power and exploitation. Literary criticism must employ class analysis, must describe and place the writers of the past with respect for all the qualities that have bound them to the just aspirations of the whole people.

As they come to know the real condition of society, writers will move into areas currently very shakily dealt with. They will deal with the subjects of anti-imperialism and anti-colonialism, for instance. Once again, that does not mean they will write political/economic tract novels, but that they will freely inhabit the full implications of anti-imperialism and anti-colonialism in Canada *in order to* develop characters and actions fully and faithfully. Writers will find a way to make imperialism, colonialism, and capitalist oppression and waste utterly present and dramatically important to a large audience. When writers know the real structures of Canadian society, theatre in Canada, for instance, will change radically. It will cease to exist as we know it, and it will become a dynamic instrument of evolutionary transformation.

As we move across this landscape of shadows towards the light, we must have compassion for one another in the struggle, even while demanding everything of each other. For we are a people who are drugged, dragooned, down-trodden, dominated and nearly drowned in the false consciousness of a colonial dependency in a bourgeois, capitalist, imperial system. To come to know the literature of this country is an act towards developing a language of struggle; it is an anti-colonial act. To know our literature in a true relation to the real structures and history of this country, to clear away by class analysis the wreckage of false consciousness strewn upon the shores of our identity and condition, to help our writers open up the possibilities of subject and treatment, to re-define the meaning of avant-garde for them, to write about and to write the literature of struggle – all those are absolute necessities, all anti-colonial acts, and all must go on at the same time.

But let me close with a strong statement about our tradition. Rightly handled, none of our literature would be dismissed. All would be properly understood, placed, and provided for. The roots of anything that we can do as a people are present in the developing psyche and consciousness of our people. That does not mean we wholly approve of our literature, but like ourselves it has happened and is here. And like ourselves it is all we've got. We could let a foreign literature define us, and, therefore, the terms of our struggle, just as we could let a foreign people liberate us from our present condition, but after a brief glance at history neither possibility seems very attractive to me or very desirable as a way of developing a language of struggle, developing the struggle, and winning the final anti-colonial struggle here, with and for the Canadian people.

Notes

1. George Grant, "Canadian Fate and Imperialism" *Technology and Empire* (Toronto: House of Anansi, 1969).

2. Works such as *The Confessions of an Immigrant's Daughter*, a novel largely about immigrant exploitation written by Laura Goodman Salverson, or *Crackpot* by Adele Wiseman, a story of a whore's life in Winnipeg, or *Barometer Rising*, by Hugh MacLennan, an attempt to define the drama and difficulty of decolonization.

THE PRODUCTION OF CANADIAN LITERATURE

JOHN FRASER

In modern capitalist society, literary culture no longer plays a direct role in supporting the leadership and dominance of the ruling class. Rather, it serves to maintain a passive acceptance of the status quo. As literary culture shifts from being a politically sensitive appendage of the bourgeousie to becoming an industry within the productive structure of society, issues of material production and consumption predominate over the more ideological and critical functions of literature. Thus, there is a movement away from conditions of competitive and semi-autonomous production to the industrialization of production and the "commodification"[1] of literature. Consequently, with the advent of modern capitalism, we can witness the decline of "independent" literary intellectuals on whom a social mandate has been bestowed – namely, the responsibility for creating imaginative reflections, not merely of, but for, society.

The writer today has thus become wholly dependent on the interlocking cultural and educational industries, which in turn rely on the ready availability of massive quantities of cultural products. These industries require from their mass audience only a superficial and subjective identification with the dominant values in society. No pre-existing identification with the social structure is required. The commodification of literature thereby ensures the cultural impoverishment of the reader, who accepts the values propagated in literature as given, and is unable to realize his actual or potential role in society. As for the writer, commodification imposes increasingly dependent status; he is obliged at one and the same time to work in industrial conditions of production, and to recognize that as an individual he is marginal and dispensible within the production process.

In the context of this pattern of evolution, Canadian writers have been unable to devise any successful counter-measures. The weakness of their present-day response indeed stems from the early phasing out of Canadian literary intellectuals in the between-wars period at the hands of the international cultural industry. The intellectual of the 1960's saw his counterpart of the pre-war years as very much his opposite; rural and parochial, as opposed to urban and national, he seemed very much a marginal figure within Canadian society and its marketplace. An interesting paradox arose, however, in that the post-war intellectuals were only capable of proposing a revival of *national* competitive capitalism which was anachronistic within the context of a predominantly neo-capitalist, *monopoly* system of production which is supranational. This attempt to open up a potential national market was in turn confused with the search for a national intellectual function at the time. In short, the opening up of a national market was falsely conceived as an adequate strategy of resistance to the writer's growing stance of powerlessness and economic marginality within the cultural industry. This response to the internationalism of the cultural market and its commodities had clearly become riddled with ambiguities and perplexities by the mid-1970's. Monopoly capitalism has had no difficulty in absorbing the nationalist Canadian literature by expanding its own economic activity. Simultaneously, it can absorb the pre-(or paleo-) capitalist *themes* of much contemporary Canadian literature without risk. These themes have been accompanied by nostalgia for the status of the "traditional literary intellectual," for although the new writer claims to seek a broader more "democratic base" than his colonial or European ancestor, he tries to emulate his social function and social mandate – despite the break with the older traditions.

The new literary intellectuals present no threat to the cultural industry. However, there exists an important difference between the old and new Canadian intellectual which clearly expresses a change in social function. The new literary intellectual's social mandate, if recognized, will be blessed by the patron state as well as by the industry. This success may confer on the writer international status and distribution, but, paradoxically, it will be seen as a betrayal of his specifically national audience and industry.

Faced with these constricted and equivocal choices, Canadian writers seem unable to conceive of a viable future, either capitalist or socialist. Very often this issue is explained away, couched in traditional liberal terms, by pointing out the inherent incompatibility of artistic independence with state or industry dependence. It appears that the Canadian writer is acutely aware of the limitations imposed by this dependence – both his own, and that of the new middle strata which form his audience. This shared dependence is the one organic link between the writer and his audience. Both share a sense of powerlessness and certain characteristics of economic exploitation. Thus, the Canadian writer has no special reason to legitimate the status quo – except, of course, when he is editor, publisher, or publicist as well as writer. Even though he may try to present society as a whole, the only real community with his audience rests on those elements of status he shares in common with his audience. It is the cultural industry itself that determines the nature of the writer's relationship, and thereby his immediate reality, with the reader as consumer – a responsibility formerly guarded with jealousy by the traditional literary intellectual (if never with authentic autonomy).

Canadian writers lack political prestige, and in any case there are evident limits to the efficacy of any form of *literary* protest. This powerlessness derives not merely from the process of cultural impoverishment or destitution of which they are more or less unwilling accomplices, but also from their position as non-salaried, contractual and non-wage labour in the industry. In addition, greater prestige and power in Canada have always been conferred on other intellectual categories – especially the administrative and the technical intellectual. The phasing out of the earlier parochial intellectual was essentially that of a local figure. The advent of modern capitalism means that literature has become an adjunct of the leisure industries, operating on an international scale—a passive pastime, for enjoyment in consumption as opposed to production time. It would appear that, given that successful national development leads only to multinational diffusion of Canadian literature, the only real choice of the writer who wishes to resist his dependent economic situation involves accentuating his political, and therefore, ideological dependence on the patron state.

In the light of the statements just made, we may begin in this chapter to ask the question: what are the consequences of neo-capitalist development on the one hand and commodification of Canadian literature on the other, and how do these relate to the possibility of effective resistance? An attempt can also be made to analyse the significance of these themes, not merely as they reflect society, but as they penetrate the contradictions of that society.

The End of the Traditional Intellectual

Present-day attempts to insert Canadian literature into the educational industry (as well as the ideological apparatus of the state in general), on the basis of this literature's forming part of a continuous literary tradition, are futile and nostalgic. In Europe and the U.S.A., by the end of the 1950's, the "isolation of mystery" of the writer had already been effectively destroyed. The pre-war Canadian literary intellectual was not a critical, cosmopolitan figure in the American or European mould. Like his counterpart today, he lacked a sense of technical affinity with the mainstream experimental literature. He also lacked a clear sense of social identity, or to be more precise, an identification with the dynamic forces of economic and political development and their social agents and victims. In short, the traditional literary intellectual was not destroyed in Canada by the cultural industry, since he had never existed in the first place. Attempts to re-capture the traditional and relatively active part played by nineteenth-century intellectuals are as hopeless and irrelevant as attempts in the structure of the industry to re-capture competitive capitalism in monopoly capitalist conditions. Ideology has been effectively relegated to a subordinate role, that of encouraging acceptance and consumption of capitalist hegemonic *values* in the form of *commodities*. When literature ceased to be a "relatively autonomous element of the superstructure" it ceased to modify and elaborate the *ideological* dominance of the ruling class. The subordination of that literature has in turn come to be a *necessity* of ideological dominance. The contemporary function of literature lies in reinforcing dominant values in the form of encouraging enjoyment and the recognition of the hegemony of dominant values as a pastime, contingent on the subordination of autonomous and critical literature. The new writer serves the economic form of that dominance.

For a short period in the late 1960's, Canadian intellectuals were called to fill a traditional role, that of the ideological elaboration and cementing of bourgeois dominance. The old function of the intellectual in society as the one who "produces novelty for society" has harnessed to the state campaign to differentiate the Canadian economic and ideological structure from that of the United States. However, the strategy was short-lived. In effect, the new literary intellectual continued to undergo the process of economic subordination usually referred to as proletarization. This process does not imply that the writer need necessarily feel himself to be a member of the proletariat. In economic terms, in fact, his relationship to the industry is more akin to that of a migrant or seasonal worker than a wage-earning employee. His relationship is predominantly a contractual one. He may also serve as a functionary of the cultural or educational industries, and though as *writer* he is a worker engaged in unproductive but necessary labour, his position also contains elements of professional autonomy. In short, he retains some characteristics of professional status, along with other characteristics of economic backwardness akin to that of the domestic worker.

The new Canadian intellectual embodies many contradictory and incompatible roles in one. However, he does not represent continuity with the pre-war intellectual, nor with the function of the critical intellectual in the nineteenth-century tradition of bourgeois realism.[2]

Canadian Literature in the 1960's

Under modern capitalism, Canada had developed as a tributary or secondary market with its indigenous literary production pushed into obscurity. With the decline by the 1950's of the old intellectual, for whom writing was perforce a recondite hobby, marginal to the social and political concerns of the ruling class, the 1960's produced a new *dependent* intellectual who understood the strategy of contestation (a 1960's term), without the experience of commitment. This complete break in continuity with the native tradition and the cultural evolution of Europe and the U.S.A. was accompanied by the use of competitive, small scale capitalist production as a vehicle of cultural diffisuion.

Since the mid-1960's we can discern two phases. The first phase, from 1965 to 1971, was extensive and often radical. Economically favourable conditions masked the rickety and regressive nature of the economic structure of the Canadian publishing industry. Since 1971, however, there has been a recessional and defensive phase, with multinational and state enterprise moving in to formalize relations between the new writer and his audience, and to support the native industry. The motives for this were often explicitly political – to boost Canadian literary production for spurious national ends – for instance, those of monolingualism or federalism. The audience of the 1960's was essentially educated in rapidly expanding and often new universities, employed in service and state (especially educational) enterprises. These were essentially workers in the tertiary sector of the economy and they had failed by the early 1970's to uphold their earlier radical promise. However, they remained potentially a politically sensitive element. In the 1960's, the new tertiary workers did indeed seem a *national* phenomenon. The radical anti-imperialism and anti-Americanism of the late 1960's seemed to offer this crucial stratum a clear distinction from the traditional working class represented by international unions, and from traditional productive workers in general.

In practice, despite the nationalist rhetoric of the period, the workers in the tertiary sector were conformist and insecure.

The new writers themselves were of socially mixed origin, but more typically products of narrow and conservative literary grouping, hence unable to provide perspectives and objectives to what was, at best, the most rootless and self-conscious stratum of modern capitalist society. The state moved from a mood of caution, and some apprehension, to a relieved acceptance by the 1970's of the political immaturity and economic desperation of these writers. In other words, the success of securing the new literature to forms acceptable to capitalist and state enterprises was not due merely to co-option, rather it marked the historical and economic limitations of the writers and their audience.

National-Popular or "Mass" Literature?

The new literary intellectuals often referred, consciously or not, to the concept of a national-popular character of literature set out by the Marxist theorist Gramsci. Gramsci was most concerned with the function of the intellectual as a cement of diverse social forces. National-popular literature is open to many interpretations. To many writers, to be national-popular is a means of overcoming the isolation and alienation of the writer in bourgeois society. The critical realism of, for example, Balzac was not the mark of an alienated writer. Balzac had elaborated the critical tensions of bourgeois society, and Zola had pushed this critique to its limits, from within the terms of that society. After Zola, it was clear that not only the proletariat but also the writer, in certain respects, experiences alienation within a capitalist society. To many people, therefore, national-popular literature serves as both a way back to nineteenth-century critical realist function, as well as to a mass audience. In fact, it would be a mistake to view the national-popular writer as an inheritor of the mass audience for the cultural industry. National-popular is not a combination of nationalist and populist as many Canadian writers in search of their elusive social mandate seem to think. When Gramsci himself used the term, he referred to Shakespeare and the Greek tragedians, not to the populist (independent petit-bourgeois) nor to the subaltern (folklore) cultures. The dream of the new Canadian literature, of becoming both national and popular, faded before recession, the obvious powerlessness and aimlessness of the new salariat class, and the fragility of the Canadian publishing industry.

Intellectually, there was no resurgence, no fresh injection, of cultural influence in the 1970's. Instead of taking a message to the people, Canadian writers started in the 1970's to stress the themes of privacy and disillusion, and began to address themselves to issues presented by society, rather than those suppressed and hidden from it.

The narrow base of intellectual influence, mentioned earlier, was not significantly broadened. The definition of culture derived from Frazer and Jung. The academic and eclectic distillations of Elliot, Joyce, Woolf, Lessing, Brecht, Voznesensky – even on to Idries Shah and Heidegger – could have been compiled in the late 1960's. Rejected by a mass audience (save under the compulsion of academic English studies) Canadian literature had come to rely on supportive critics to provide it with buying audience.

The failure of the protest movement of the late 1960's to find adequate organizational forms had led to two tendencies by the mid-1970's – when the first major quantitative expansion of Canadian literature took place. On the other hand, there was an increased dependence on the spectacle, namely poetry reading, the weekend magazine, the publicity article or review used to promote, on the interviewers' terms, a "literary" cause. On the other side, there developed a reaction to this use of the media for educational purposes, with its more explicit political message. Canadians were not used to identifying with this particular approach. Behind the media as well there lay the state with its particular interest in maintaining a centralized and responsive communications industry. Writers became disillusioned with their readers in the tertiary sector. Art as an autonomous sphere of activity appeared once more to be the order of the day. This tendency, of course, confused the issue of cultural autonomy with that of political autonomy. It also confused the economic question of the "national market" with the "national-popular" programme with all its many variants.

Commodification

The commodification of cultural products makes the writer dependent on his industry, whatever his background and however attached to the dominant values of that society. The fact that these values may be bourgeois in a bourgeois society does not, of course, vary the relation of dependency. It is the industry alone that makes possible a relationship with the public. It is only through the industry that the public establishes some contact with the writer. In accepting responsibility for this relationship, the industry in a sense absolves the writer of any other responsibility – indeed, deprives him of it. The writer has the option of resisting outside the industry, and hence be unpublished – effectively a non-writer – or he can resist ineffectively from within.

The reader is a buyer, and the writer a seller. The market is as elastic as any other commodity market. However, it is not a market of ideas but one of commodities, and its freedom one of things not ideas. Despite this, one should be careful not to see the cultural industry as the end of culture, but rather as a new culture. One must reject the argument which states that the commodification of a product and the creation of a mass audience dictates an *absolute* tendency to the homogenization of market and product. Monopoly capital can develop specialist as well as mass audiences.

It is also hard to agree that the de-sanctification of art by technical reproduction, the ending of its ritualistic character and its replacement by a potentially democratic character, have the immediate political potential that Benjamin hoped for – that of democratizing mass art.[3] Still less can one accept Enzensberger's optimistic thought that every new cultural medium has its subversive counter-use, an automatic counterpart to every capitalist use of the technique.[4] It is through the assumption of the responsibility for mediating the relationship of writer to society that the cultural industry assumes control of the leisure time of the reader and the productive time of the writer. In this way, by determining the form of the product, the content is also determined.

From Intellectuals to a National Intelligentsia

According to Gramsci, the traditional intellectual performed an ideological role within the social superstructure. The proletariat emerging in the early stages of industrialization had to rely on the defection of traditional intellectuals and their integration within a political system not closely integrated with the new productive forces. These pre-industrial intellectuals would, as it was hoped, rapidly be replaced by proletarian intellectuals. When considering the cultural industry in conditions of modern capitalism, however, the Gramscian picture changes. Populist realism is itself an inadequate means of portraying the new reality. The intellectual loses his position of shared dominance beside the active, directing bourgeois. Despite his complete subordinance to the cultural industry, the writer is constrained to play a traditional role to the new intelligentsia. Although, as in Italy today, the mass of the population has started to reject bourgeois hegemony, the literary intellectual has little effective power. However, he is not totally powerless within his industry, and, through this, in his relationship to society. In this situation, other politically radical intellectuals (technical, administrative, teaching) may be better able to act as spokesmen for the proletariat through their greater political and organizational influence. In Canada a challenge to bourgeois hegemony on this scale has yet to be made. At present, the writer fulfils the *technical* role of literary intellectual, but is himself, along with the industry he serves, a function of the development of the new intelligentsia whose inherent limitations and partial nature he shares.

There are thus deep causes of separation between literary intellectuals and intelligentsia, in consequence between writer and society at large. At the same time, there are vital meeting points: writers, as we have seen, undergo forms of exploitation within industrial production, and as part of "labour-power in process of formation" undergo a process common to the majority of intelligentsia, a transformation not based on privileged or traditional educational formation. Out of this common meeting ground there are various starting points from which writers can experiment with differing forms of contestation that are not elitist. Forms of experimental language, for example, or the limited but real ability of several U.S. writers to influence the social and political mores. The use of certain forms of experimental language effectively asserts the need to reject the norms of bourgeois language and its functional relation with bourgeois reality, so-called ordinary life. The rejection of the norms of ordinary language does not, of course, necessarily infer the rejection of reality, but can open the way to postulating different forms of alternate realities.[5]

The values propagated by the cultural industry are those of the status quo, and bear no direct relation to hegemony or moral commitment. The cultural industry is quick to diffuse the effects of inventive, experimental literary forms by establishing competition between essentially similar objects[6], and is not concerned with establishing a hierarchy of factional tastes, or partisan audiences. Thus, although experimental and avant-garde forms of literature are constantly open to co-option by the industry, it is a mistake to define them as being unequivocally reactionary.

Europe in the 1960's seemed to offer only two choices to the intellectual – that of becoming a literary, protesting intellectual working through a review or literary group, or else the task of becoming a political militant who, in fact, ceased to function as an intellectual. Nowadays, one can see different types of intellectuals organizing and conscious of their role within modern capitalism, even to the extent of dropping the term intellectual altogether on the grounds that intellectuals are no longer separate from the process of material production, and hence have no real distinguishing characteristics as a group. It is therefore important to keep in mind that when we speak of the limitations of literary intellectuals, we are not concerned with a static, rigidly defined group, but one that is in constant flux and change. Mental workers in general are not reducible to the humanistic, political, cultural and directive functions of the traditional intellectual. The strategies of contestation need not, on principle, therefore reject intellectuals because of the social equivocation of the traditional literary intellectual.

The Continuity of the Literary Intellectual

The problem remains that in Canada, as elsewhere, literary intellectuals retain a privileged position. They may be incarcerated within "ivory towers," even at their own request, but they are not popularly supposed to be wholly indifferent to public issues. As Butor has commented, in scientific and technical writing there exists simply the writer and reader, whereas in literature there is the writer, the reader, and the hero.[7] The cultural industry, however, tries to reduce the ground on which writer and reader meet to that of a neutral zone, of gratuitous information which is above suspicion precisely because it is gratuitous – in other words, providing the satisfaction "of a need one did not know one had."

Despite this, Canadian writers have areas for debate on contestation they have yet to explore fully. Canadian writers have generally been convinced that they should be on the level with their readers proposed by their industry, and that the focal point for determining the ideological relationship between writer and society should and could only be the industry, whether national or monopoly. No room exists of course, for the autonomous writer within the industry, but there may still be space outside for different kinds of activity. The national market clearly provides no base for political unity. Thus, the missing subject of Canadian literature is not the "nation" but literary culture itself. The elusive antagonist is not that all-pervasive and oppressive force which is seldom named but clearly known to be the U.S.A., nor is it anthropomorphized natural forces, as spelled out in arcane critical themes. Rather, the unidentified antagonist is the cultural industry, and the part it plays in eroding quality and skills and devaluing the critical intellect.

Fundamental choices clearly emerge for the writer; between being a writer in the true sense and being an entrepreneur within the cultural industry, between the application of Canadian literature as a token sector of the Canadian industry (Canadiana), and genuine resistance to exploitation. In the 1960's, the confusion of spectacle with promotion and publicity, cultural with political unity, and literary with political protest, was not unfruitful. As a result of the crisis, Canadian intellectuals became integrated as a cohesive group within the economy. The current decline of this mood of crisis, however, has led to a belief that the crisis existed only within the literary tradition itself. This belief is a result of inadequate analysis and reflection on the international roots of Canadian literature and its audience. The response of Canadian writers has been over-specialist and limited. They have tended to concentrate on questions which become almost conundrums. Can a national state-aided capitalist enterprise transcend the internal disunity of Canada? Can a monolinguist literature overcome not only the existence of two distinct national cultures, but also numerous, embryonic ethnic literatures, especially when this national literature is in dire competition with two overwhelmingly powerful international literatures?

The Latest Phase

By the early 1970's the conflict between economic and cultural autonomy was obvious. The former was national-capitalist, the latter anti-monopoly, two concepts with no meeting ground save on the most superficial level. Despite this, writers were, by and large, unable to define the function they could fulfil in society, and could not perceive how their subordination could be reconciled to the task of creating a national base with their principle audience, the new tertiary workers. The literature which in the 1960's had been both progressive and nostalgic – in Canadian terms, therefore, social-democratic – began to express itself increasingly in the terms of laissez-faire, or private and individual enterprise. Cosmopolitanism was also rejected within this new trend, and outrage was expressed against the degradation of the writer by the exigencies of the economy.

Clearly, the choice between remaining a leisure-time cultural functionary or acting as a mere spokesman for the reformist wing of the bourgeoisie was unattractive. But it was the only choice offered by the Canadian publishing industry, as opposed to the elastic and passive reactions of the monopoly sector (which were often prepared to offer better financial rewards to the writer). There is no doubt that Canadian literature had established important links within such institutions as schools and universities, and to a lesser extent within the government. It had certainly not achieved a public face, or generated the debate and public excitement originally hoped for. The reasons for this are not hard to find. There was a marked contradiction in the *national* resurgence of literature created on the backs of dependent writers, fiercely competing for attention and support from various governments and the cultural industry. The bourgeoisie required the creation of this literature not for their own consumption but for propagation to other classes. Literature was held to be, in any event, an enclosed, specialist subject. Talk of "cultural imperialism" was a slogan of slight conviction, in view of Middle America's stifling indifference to intellectual sophistication. The truth of the matter was that the debate in essence was virtually indistinguishable from aspects of cultural impoverishment in general – indeed, nowhere more extreme than within the American heartland itself. Canadian literature was unable to devise alternative forms. The Canadian best-seller must perforce confine itself to the general rules of the genre. The failure to devise a positive political or cultural line, or to relate this failure to actual conditions within the industry or in production at large, threw writers back onto a thin defence. Ironically, the argument that it was monopoly that had deprived Canadians of their heritage served only to encourage monopolies to fill the gap in their lists.

It would, of course, be absurd to dismiss the phenomenon of new Canadian literature as a mere spasm of monopoly capital, and to see the current difficulties of Canadian writers as merely the result of indifferences to culture inherited from previous generations. It would be unwise to welcome the end of the pretensions of the traditional literary intellectual and his efforts towards proletarization with a sentimental or moralistic attitude. These tendencies, however, do really exist, and Canadian writers have not been particularly quick to recognize and react to them.

Outside Canada, the end or temporary eclipse of the traditional literary intellectual has given rise to many strategic suggestions. At first there were attempts to organize writers within politically autonomous, though still implicitly political, groups. Those intellectuals who had lost their role as advisers to the ruling class (from which their new-found "autonomy" sprang), sought a similar role with regard to the proletariat and its political parties. Their desire was for a "separateness," combined with their essential commitment. These changes tended to give rise to hard and fast cliques, sectarian rather than autonomous in nature. Only during the late 1960's was the distinction between the old-guard intellectuals and intelligentsia brought into the open. Only after 1969 did intelligentsia, and "intellectual labour power in formation" seek political organization (for instance through the Italian Communist Party) as a unifying base. In Canada, of course, the national experience of the 1960's and the contingent upheaval of the late 1960's were either lacking entirely, or only very slightly in evidence.

The Gains of the 1960's in Canada

Writers did come to make some major discoveries in the 1960's, however, and first amongst these was the fact that their alienation could be attributed principally to their general subordination to the cultural industry. It is not so much that the bourgeoisie dictated what the writer must write, but rather that the writer could feel a tangible and general subordination to the cultural industry. Also, it has to be realized that modern capitalism acknowledges the categorization of intellectual labour in an unprecedented manner. "Labour power in formation" through universal education is a preparation for the situation in which the "collective labourer" becomes increasingly intellectualized, and the balance turns in favour of the intellectual as opposed to manual function. However, the intellectualization of labour power is in fact socio-economic in character, as opposed to political or cultural. It does not offer the specialist intellectual any vast new range of activities and influence, because the overall intellectualization takes place in and for the process of material production. The new intelligentsia did not automatically provide the Canadian writer with an audience of higher cultural and political consciousness.

It can therefore be seen that the notion of retaining individual "autonomous" enterprise in literature is invalid under the new conditions of industrialization and socialization of intellectual labour. Within capitalist society, competitiveness destroys effectively the co-operative potential of this socialization, and leads to ever higher levels of individual competition, hand-in-hand with the ideology of individual autonomy. It has been said that achievement of artistic success by "speculative operations on a vast scale," in which the artist is "promoted and strictly controlled by the big marketing corporations," means that "it is almost impossible for anyone not in line with current artistic tendencies to hope to be successful, or to be 'discovered'."[8] Thus, even literature written with the specific intention of changing the imaginative topography of society is subject to, and shaped by, identical pressures. The classic example of the total subordination, and by implication social ambition, of the literary producer is the Best Seller. This is defined not so much by qualitative cultural influence, rather by the success of its sales.

It must be recognized that in Canada the notion of "national culture" is not a descriptive but ideological one, and that the attempts to depart from a marginal and localized status rest on the shaky conception of what constitutes a national-popular intellectual. The rise of a class of humanistically educated high-school and university graduates has to be clearly distinguished from the particular form of the national cultural industry produced for them, and in large part produced by this class. The trinity of writer, teacher and publisher can no longer serve at one and the same time the evidently mutually exclusive ends of economic and ideological nationalism. State aid alone has maintained some semblance of unity between the intellectual and political demand for autonomy, and the competitive, economic autonomy desired by the Canadian publishing industry. This vital connection, indeed umbilical cord, cannot be too strongly stressed. In the 1970's the humanistically educated graduate feels threatened and divided from his peers – above all from his government. Neither potential audience nor writers can fully accept that the Canadian national culture should be, indeed, economically has to be, a state-supported, even official, ideology.

State support immediately raises the question of the function of literature in modern capitalist society. What justification is there to support a "high" literature modelled on the literatures of "cultural imperialism," and directed to a small part of what is already a minority audience for this literature? Surely a genuinely popular literature would require no support, and would automatically assume monopoly forms? On the other hand, a really national-popular literature would surely shun the traditional channels of diffusion employed by the publishing industry. But it is clear that Canadian literature, in accepting that it needed special help to become popular, had no intention of changing its form. Its practitioners, by and large, accepted the historic mission of later bourgeois writers, namely that of continuing the bourgeois cultural tradition. To this end, the "new audience" was simply a product of the educational industry acting in collusion with the college books division of the publishing industry. Thus, despite the rhetoric and spectacle of publicity surrounding new or much-promoted authors, the literature relied heavily on forms and themes already legitimated by "high" culture. To put this negative judgement in comparative perspective, it is only fair to point out the relative failure of any group of European intellectuals to break the mould of traditional literature and monopoly, and to establish genuinely national-popular connections.[9]

The national-popular element in Canada was essentially an attempt to discover a forgotten tradition, to make a voyage of discovery not so much to an empty continent, but to one peopled by noble aborigines. This adaptation of romantic English liberalism was deaf both to the American avant-garde and the extensive European debate on the subordination of the writer within the cultural industry. In education, the insertion of Canadian literary works to substitute for, or complement, the established British or American books was at worst a reactionary reliance on the academic and class authority of the teacher and the publicist to "sell Canadian." At best, it was a limited and timid attempt to pose the question of why it was at all necessary to revive a form of literature in crisis, which was neither popular nor national and which, above all, was marginal, given the inability or reluctance of the working class to consume cultural products.

Culture takes many forms, and functions at different levels within different societies. In Canada, despite the tendency of literature to be removed from the sphere of intellectual action to that of the mere filling of leisure time, the new literature retained much of the ideology of the old, independent petit bourgeois as a literary *theme*. This theme was anachronistic and nostalgic in relation to the new, dependent petite bourgeoisie. Although there may be an analogy between the older petit-bourgeois radicalism and populism, and certain aspects of the new radicalism, this latter lacked historical awareness of the limits of the analogy. In particular it retained no understanding of, or interest in, the relationship between their historical origin and their present situation. Even present-day attempts at writing "critical history" are addressed to a group which conceives of the past in terms of nobility, a golden age – and has no historical reference point except that offered by the media. The new petit bourgeois retains no organizational framework and institutional memory, whilst Canadian literature offers a political and ideological, not an affective, attachment to a particular view of community. Despite the fact that the new literature proposed a definition of the national community somewhat more sophisticated than that possessed by its audience, the new writers themselves shared traits of dependency with their audience. They accepted a traditional role – that of the powerless elite of the cultural industry. Although they challenged the colourless and conformist view of Canadian history, they did so as dependents writing for dependents.

Aims of the Canadian Writer

The idea of a nationally inspired, community-resolved class struggle avoided the very questions most affecting the writer unable to make a living and identify his audience. It also obscured problems of radically altering the function of popular literature. It is true that Canadian writers were anxious to come to terms with the non-literary and relatively unsophisticated character of their society, similar in many ways to the American experience of cultural destitution. They did this, however, by attempting to recapture a pre-literary tone, enterprising, but now effectively destroyed. This approach was scarcely compatible with the desire to arouse, not merely to entertain, the new national middle strata. Writers in fact found themselves torn between two narrow perspectives. The first was an historical "vertical" narrowness, in which literature does not fulfil any central organic role but stresses the continuity of a part of society through the medium of a mythical, external and detached level of common reference. The other perspective was a parallel horizontal narrowness, that of the new middle class to whose cultural pretensions those social classes above and below them remained largely indifferent – expressing the ahistorical homogeneity of a broad stratum of society.

Despite their lack of belief in a viable future, Canadian writers presented these limited visions within the romantic context of a belief that the quality of a nation is reflected in its culture, irrespective of the conditions in which it is produced. The literature of the vertical or horizontal stratum was produced in peculiar conditions. Although, in the strict Marxist sense, writers are engaged in commodity production, and hence the producers of surplus value and exploited as proletarians, they are not normally employed as wage labour by the Canadian cultural industry. As producers, they act in the same form as early industrial domestic workers. Consequently, it is not at all surprising that common Canadian themes in literature are marginality, indirect and primitive forms of exploitation, and a search for pre-capitalist community.

Of course, it may be objected that creative writers in general are not strictly wage labourers. In Canada, however, we find a meeting ground between the broad themes of national development, the socio-economic position of the contemporary writer, and that of the conditions of the publishing industry. The historically legitimate theme of seeking community, however small, even when personalized into communities of one or two, finds an immediate contemporary relevance in the writers' own conditions of production. The Canadian writer here is peculiarly dependent on the ideology of the industry he serves. The Canadian industry has always claimed to have created the Canadian writer, provided him with a public and a national cultural role. However, the fact that the conditions of production provided for the majority of Canadian writers remain anarchic, archaic and, indeed, chaotic is a truism.

The industry can blame the dependency and powerlessness of the writer on the simple fickleness of a non-reading public. This does not take into account the gap between the pretentious claim to national status and the precarious position of the artist, given that the latter sanctions the dependence of the writer on the industry. Consequently, the undertones of hopelessness, suffocation and marginality may be traced not only to the traditional characteristics of the Canadian writer, but to his failure to find organizational form for a new definition of literature in society.

Canadian literature, in short, had to be new and modern, but had also to fill a gap. It had to satisfy the ambition of the writer, to be the re-creation of an absent phenomenon, a national literature of the type elsewhere subordinated to monopoly. The actual depressed *social* condition of the literary intellectual was in sharp contrast to what appeared to be his *historical* mandate, namely that of writing a missing literature and supplying a body of pre-industrial traditions. The Canadian writer was called upon to transcend the parochial condition of earlier Canadian literature by writing for a national audience which, as we have noted, was not one which at any point overcame the hostility and indifference to or incomprehension of "high culture" in the working mass of the population. In short, this national literature became simply an updated and structurally restricted version of the old parochialism – in sharp contrast to the perspective of other types of contemporary intellectuals, technical and administrative, which was overwhelmingly international and cosmopolitan.

The theme of the threat to culture from industry in general, and that of the irresolvable conflict between public expectations and private sensibilities, illustrates the equivocal and synthetic position of the Canadian writer. Canadian literature was at one and the same time too insecure and too traditional to have discovered in "its own" publishing houses a strategy of resistance to monopoly capitalism. There can be no autonomous solution to the problem – by politico-cultural reviews and groups, or by experimentalism and the avantgarde. In fact, the alienation of the critical writer from bourgeois society has been intensified as much as the alienation of the critical writer from "popular society." Commodification subordinates the relation of writer-society to the habits of leisure-time consumption. In class society, these habits are stronger and more vigorously reinforced than those fostered by the educational system which, despite an ideology of classlessness, operates as a mechanism for the selection and legitimation of dominant values.

Already we can see a confluence of monopoly and national enterprise. Instead of a community of national literary intellectuals, local schools or coteries on the American model have developed. The lyric has re-asserted itself over the epic. The novel has failed to find a new and organic form. Those literary intellectuals who perceive their loss of status and function and refuse to compromise for the sake of commercial popularity are marginal, even to those who share their understanding of the problem. This is because the problem of literary culture is not resolvable by literary means alone. Culture is politics, and politics culture – but at present Canadian culture is not recognized as a potentially effective practice of politics.

In Quebec, by contrast, although the material condition of the francophone writer is substantially the same as that of the anglophone counterpart, the function of the literary intellectual has a political substance lacking elsewhere in Canada. Dependence on the state changes its meaning when a possibility of changing the state emerges. Relations with the "masses" are different when there are mass organizations whose radical or reformist aims are partly those of articulating new and active relationships between the classes of mental and manual labour. Elsewhere, however, there has risen a dominant belief in the integrative power of the national-popular tradition acting as a re-creation of the moribund traditional intellectual, combined with the American notion of culture as functional training for citizenship.

In Canadian literature, the success of the writer follows the power of the industry. Successful organization of the industry provides the only terrain for the success of the writer. Canadian writers have, in the past decade, concentrated on many forms of exploitation – women, nature, oneself (as *savoir faire/savoir vivre*). With few exceptions, however, the theme of the exploitation of living labour as the central *humanist* theme of resistance to capitalism has been avoided. It may be said that the other forms of exploitation refer in a figurative sense to the capitalist one. Nevertheless, when the writers are not speaking figuratively but as public figures, they do not, by and large, take up the theme of capitalism exploitation. They may indeed reject cultural imperialism as an integral part of imperialism. As Canadian writers, however, they are increasingly absorbed into the economic structure of imperialism. They become a sub-group of its agents, interested in overcoming problems of localism and parochialism, and of expanding the audience for "high" literature.

The concern of Canadian literature, in short, is with the conquest of a literary, rather than a political or social space. Yet this literary concern does of course admit a particular acceptance of the de-politicization of culture through its subordination to the state, and to the leisure activities of the middle class. Canadian literature is not one of shattered forms, brutality or colonial repression. The tone is controlled, cautious, optimistic, academic, syncretic, and essentially secure. It is not the literature of a society which feels itself in ferment, thus the literature itself increasingly ceases to be in ferment.

Cultural Imperialism

"Cultural imperialism" can no longer support the feeble analogy that Canada is a third-world, or even a second-world colony. The interesting question is rather why the significance of native literary intellectuals has been so slight even given cultural imperialism, whether the regaining of some relevance (accompanied by intensive exploitation of the new intellectuals) indicates a new phase of resistance. In the 1970's it became clear that Canadian literature had developed with the aid of a productive capacity whose growth had now slowed down or ceased altogether. It had possessed a narrow social base, and had followed the fortunes of a local, small and weak industry.

Three diagnoses of the historical situation of Canadian literature as reflected within literary culture have been made. First it has been suggested that Canadian cultural conservatism is a product of localism, and that the process of modernization must destroy that very particularism once felt to be the authentic form of national resistance. Secondly, a body of opinion relates the problem of culture to a lack of identity of the new "intellectual middle strata." This view sees the difficulty as one of psyche, whereas the first is ideological and geographical. The third explanation is that there has been a flight from the communitarian localism of Canadian society to a more fragmented and diffuse form, sensitive and ego-conscious, concerned with the politics of the individual.

Within the context of these diagnoses, the question of the majority, or the non-consumers of "high" or bourgeois culture, was not raised. The relationship between the spread of literary culture and that of new forms of political power was also not made. Yet, the political class which had previously reacted with indifference to literary intellectuals became intent in the late 1960's in establishing a strategic distance for itself from the United States. It gave writers in conditions of dependency the old ideological role of the traditional intellectual – that of the re-definition and justification of the new orientation of the state. The absence of a native literary culture became, in this situation, anomalous.

The interest of the state lay in the need to make ideological distinctions between the American and Canadian middle classes, and this coincided with the desire of the Canadian publishing industry to take advantage of a climate favourable for expansion. Neither the state nor the publishing industry had any real intention, or hope, of reversing monopoly control over the mass market, or changing the dominant form of culture in modern capitalist society. It is a mistake to ascribe precise motives and reasons where none are clearly thought out, or defined. It is enough simply to suggest that a national literature had economic and political advantages for the industry and the state which in many objective instances ran directly counter to the interests and objectives of the writers. A high literature is politically powerless in advanced capitalist society except in the possibility of its broad dissemination to a significant selection of intellectual labour power. Ingested within the long term, whether within mass culture or the museum, a literary culture can, in the short term, perform one of several parallel functions. It secures the loyalty of a section of the intellectuals. It creates an area of legitimacy and organic contact with a broad section of the population, especially through mass education. It acts as a social cement and means of self-identification, it also establishes the saliency of the national state as protector of the intellectual and his culture, and thence of "national identity."

Conclusion

The attempt to fulfil the function of "national identity" by presenting a traditional mythologized past did not conform to the actual conditions of the writer's audience. Nor did the literary intellectuals find effective organizational links beyond those set down and mediated by the industry. In the early 1970's intellectuals assumed the ideological function of modernizers once the need to insulate Canada both from American imperialism, and imperialism at large, had lessened.

The story of the new Canadian literature is not simply a fable of manipulation and innocence betrayed by modern capitalism, nor is it a history of contestation overtaken by economic realities. The new literary intellectual escaped none of the dilemmas, equivocations and deprivations of his obscure but less dependent predecessors. In addition, he suffered from the general post-war degradation of literature, a degradation made the more painful because of his colleagues' criticism of the politically unimaginative resources of creative literature.

A "governmental-elitist" literary intellectual is a type which belies the actual humble status of the Canadian writer. The state's pursuit of greater international autonomy cannot be seen as reversing this condition of dependency. It simply proposes an essentially supportive and justificatory role for the literature of the new Canadian middle class. Certain conclusions, however, can be drawn. In the first place, the distinction between capitalism and socialism is clearly the order of the day. Literature is produced by writers engaged in the social conditions of capitalist production, and the very existence of a diffuse literature depends on the forms of those relations. There can be no going back to the traditional humanistic-critical intellectual, and the state of current Canadian literary production shows clearly that its early promise cannot be sustained within its capitalist structure. Secondly, modern capitalism commodifies the new Canadian literature, and is hence the *determining* factor which institutes the relation of writer to audience. Finally, there has been a movement in Canadian literature away from the desire to play an active part within the superstructure to an acceptance of a role legitimating the status quo. This has been done in the name of the liberalism of the new middle petit-bourgeois – and not the *national* function which, in its many forms, the writer of the 1960's sought.

Modern Canadian literature is in acute danger of sinking into the attitudes and interests of the most rootless, the most insecure, the least historically conscious and motivated class – that of the dependent workers of the tertiary sector. It is unlikely that the present generation of Canadian writers will by themselves help to motivate and mobilize the working class – but a literary community which ignores the reality and "cultural absence" of this class has no real claim to a social mandate.

Notes

1. Refers to literature as a marketable commodity rather than existing for its own sake.

2. See L. Goldmann, *Pour une Sociologie du Roman* (Paris, 1964), and on the theory of literary production, Pierre Macherey, *Pour une Theorie de la Production Littéraire* (Paris, 1969).

3. W. Benjamin, *L'Opera d'Arte nell'Epoca della sua Riproducibilita Tecnica* (Turin, 1966).

4. H. M. Enzensberger, "Constituents of a Theory of the Media." *New Left Review*, no. 64 (November-December, 1970).

5. A. Gouldner, "Prologue to a Theory of Revolutionary Intellectuals," *Telos*, no. 26 (Winter 1975-6) on the relation between the language-capacity of intellectuals and political action.

6. F. Poli, *Produzione Artistica e Mercato* (Turin, 1975).

7. M. Butor, *Essais sur le Roman* (Paris, 1972).

8. Poli, *ibid.*

9. A. Gramsci, *Gli Intellettuali* (Turin, 1955). This work is the source of the terms "traditional intellectual" and "national-popular" used throughout.

PART 3: SOCIOLOGICAL PROBLEMS OF REGIONAL LITERATURE

INTRODUCTION
PAUL CAPPON

The problem of "regional literature" was defined in the introductory essay as one of the three immediately pressing issues for an activist sociology of Canadian literature. It is important not only in terms of the regions within Canada but also in terms of the debate surrounding a definition of English Canadian literature as part of a wider Anglo-Saxon tradition. If such a definition were equivalent to saying that Hungarian literature was part of a European tradition, or Indonesian literature part of an Asiatic tradition, the statement would be axiomatic – and useless. We have seen, however, that the "regionalizing" of Canadian literature means much more than the fact of sharing a common language with Britain and the United States: it is the cultural expression, through the importation of imperial styles and the adoption of international standards, of the subordination in the economic and socio-political spheres of the Canadian hinterland first by the British, then by the American metropolis. The recognition of this historical relationship between the economic and the cultural is the first step in the denial of regionalization. This denial in turn is critical to the establishment in Canada of what Mathews has termed "a language of struggle" against imperialist domination and the Canadian class structure with which that dominance is bound up.

In this sense of struggle, Patricia Marchak's essay on the sociological roots of regional literature in Canada is important as an affirmation that English Canada, if it can disengage itself from its colonial ties with the United States, has the potential for building a national literature founded on Canadian authors taking their own concrete material roots as a basis for their writing. She points out also that the metropolis-hinterland connection exists within Canada itself, resulting in a kind of hierarchical subordination to the U.S. through Ontario. A seeming paradox is that, only through denying Central Canadian pretensions of unifying literary style as it "unifies" the economy through its financial control, can the various regions contribute to a culture strong enough to resist American dominance and to establish a culture of national unity. Such a national culture would be established, *not through uniformity* of modes among the various regions, but rather through each region's treating in literature the concrete problems of imperial dominance and class structure as they manifest themselves in that region. Each region has unique characteristics or manifestations of overall metropolitan dominance and class structure. The lives of people in Southern Ontario industrial cities, British Columbia company towns or Maritime areas of heavy emigration are governed by the overall structure of Canadian capitalist society; *but the specific social reality corresponding to that governance takes different forms in each of the regions.* To develop in a region styles and forms appropriate to expressing that local manifestation of a generalized reality is therefore not "regionalism." Moreover, the response to local social conditions in the literature of the various regions creates a national unity among them by the recognition of common problems manifested in different ways in each area – the problems of imperialism, of capitalistic class structure and social organization and all their related problems.

A crucial problem for Canadian literature, as Marchak indicates, is therefore the blocking of American economic and cultural dominance through Central Canada. The way to terminate the metropolis-hinterland relationship with the United

States culturally as well as economically lies not in reinforcing the power of the Ontario metropolis within Canada, but through the reverse process. Regions should secure more control over the publishing of material locally produced, and develop content and styles specific to their own experiences. Otherwise they may only imitate the literature of their metropoli. Paradoxically, the more they imitate the metropoli, the more "regional" in the sense of inferior and dependent on imperial modes becomes their literature. The less they do this, the more they base their writing on the local expression of Canadian capitalist society, referring to their material roots, the more they build both a relatively autonomous literature and a language of struggle from which other regions may benefit.

GIVEN A CERTAIN LATITUDE: A (HINTERLAND) SOCIOLOGIST'S VIEW OF ANGLO-CANADIAN LITERATURE

PATRICIA MARCHAK

The certain latitude is a northern region with more similarities between Whitehorse and Winnipeg than our central heating permits us to recognize. I propose to take a certain latitude as well in treating its literature as a sociological resource, Desmond Pacey's early judgement that "...we have as yet produced no great sociological novels" notwithstanding.[1]

I won't argue that we have produced great sociological novels since 1945: I don't know what such might be. It seems to me that Pinsent's *John and the Missus* (1974) is a rich source of sociological data on company towns, and on a Newfoundland mining town in particular. Cohen's *Beautiful Losers* (1966) tells us a fair amount about urban societies in general and Montreal in particular, and is as good a sociological document as any fictional account. Even poor novels such as Garner's *A Nice Place to Visit* (1970) or Shaffer's *The Midas Compulsion* (1969) can be perversely illuminating. The latter two tell us quite a bit about Ontario's submersion in American-style small-town pornographies, and by extension about cultural colonialism. Good literature by the standards of the aesthete is rather limited in volume: much more abundant is literature for the sociologist guided by the question "What is the relationship between this document and the society within which it is produced?"

Some fiction is deliberately sociological: that is, it sets out to provide a reader with an interpretation of a particular society. If it is written with insight by a writer whose gift it is to reveal social relationships beyond everyday perceptions, it may turn out to be a good sociological novel in Pacey's terms. In that case, the reader who wants to know more about a particular society may turn to the fictional source with the question, "What does this document tell me about the society?" By implication the fictional account is taken to be a true account, one that can be relied on as a guide towards action for people who want to live in that society. If one were abruptly propelled into French society of the 1830's, one would surely want to read Balzac and Stendhal as quickly as possible in order to obtain some clues on how to survive, how to interpret, how to make sense out of apparent social chaos. Modern fiction in Canada or elsewhere may be employed in the same way, may be read as "true" accounts. An Anglophone in Montreal would read MacLennan, Cohen, Moore, Carrier, Richler, Roy, Aquin, and the others as sources of sociological information in this way.

But this is not a sociology of literature, it is a treating of literature as truth. A sociology of literature treats "truth" as a separate entity and enquires rather how it comes about that a particular society identified as that separate entity gives rise to the particular account of itself which is represented in its literature. One would not look for truth in South African novels written by insiders who are white; no more in Russian novels written by State-subsidized academicians. For a colonized or smothered culture, one is likely to understand more about the society by studying its modes of selection: what does it allow its novelists to see, what do they choose to see, how do they choose to represent what they know?

Writers of fiction most frequently hold membership in privileged groups. Most Anglo-Canadian literature before 1930, for example, was written by two groups: British visitors passing through, and Scottish Presbyterian ministers practising their vocation in the colony. Both represented the imperial empire and shared its values. The working population consisted of diverse people with many different cultural roots and values, but they did not write fiction. Why they did not write fiction is a problem in social "truth"; that they didn't is a problem in the sociology of literature, because the resulting fictional portrait of Canadian development is a highly selective and predictably inaccurate portrait.

This kind of investigation begins with an assumption that may run contrary to much of what is preached about "modern" literature. I assume that all literature is regionally specific. I don't mean it happens to be about a place: I mean its central assumptions, its modes of expression, its social and its aesthetic concerns belong somewhere but never anywhere. There is no dichotomy between regional and universal: these two terms are not opposites. A literature tells us about a society. Frequently what it tells is unintentional. It tells us about more than one society if there happens to be more than one society with similar characteristics. But whether it does or doesn't is not a reflection on the quality of the literature, it is a reflection rather on the nature of the society.

The notion that literature ought not to be regional, or the equating of regional with "narrow" and "smugly provincial" strikes me as a manifestation of successful imperialism by that culture which, being most powerful in terms of technology and economy, takes to itself the description "universal." The process is successful to the extent that the colonized believe in their own inferiority and adopt imperial standards of excellence.

Imperial cultures are not alike in their attitudes towards colonies and satellites, and there is a difference as well between these two kinds of hinterland societies. The British phase in Canada was tied to resource extraction of a very crude kind. It did not require a homogeneous population with identical consumer tastes. Indeed, such a demanding consumer population in the colony would have been a considerable inconvenience. As long as there was a workforce prepared to trap, dig, cut, or farm resources and ship them off to Britain, the social characteristics of the workers were relatively unimportant. Such an economic base allowed the British to retain racist assumptions. Their central position in the empire allowed them to attribute to themselves such superiority that assimilation was out of the question for colonial subjects. A colonial society of British expatriates could be an inferior replica. A colonial culture of non-British settlers or indigenous peoples could be, at best, an anthropological resource. Not so incidentally, British anthropologists virtually created and dominated that discipline throughout the hey-day of empire.

By contrast, American imperialism throughout the period 1945 to about 1970 in Canada aimed at absorption of foreigners, total assimilation into the melting pot. Coca-Cola and stereophonic equipment served standardized markets. As long as resources could be obtained in many places as well as Canada, and as long as Canada financed the growth of American branch-plants and subsidiaries within its heartland, the advantages of a homogenized consumer population were best gained by treating Canadians as if, by golly, they were really Americans. The American version of anthropology was sociology – value-free, morally neutral, universalistic, concentrated on individual psychological characteristics, and dedicated to helping industry obtain a disciplined and co-operative work force.

These two faces of imperialism have both treated indigenous and distinctive regional cultures with disdain, and over the long run both tend to smother cultural diversity. The British smothered it with condescension and paternalism; the Americans with the façade of equality. In the long run, too, the colonialized have accepted alien definitions of excellence by which they misjudge their own potentialities. Nonetheless, there are significant differences in the particular forms these results take. The British phase produced a culture which was deliberately imitative, and in which potential sources of diversity – such as imported cultures of non-British settlers – were silenced by isolation.

The American period has produced a much richer mixture, in part because it did not isolate the diverse cultures along racial lines, and thus permitted contrasts to be recognized; in part because it affected different regions of the country in different ways and with diverse effects. Canadian literature throughout the past thirty years of intensive economic penetration has included an interesting variety of deliberate and unapologetic regional novelists.

It has, of course, produced others as well, and a host of urban critics who speak of regionalism as a phase to be gotten over. One of these by way of example introduced Sheila Watson's *The Double Hook* (1959) in these terms: the "ethnic-group novel" is "essentially condescending to the people it describes" and therefore "not universal or even fully human, since the basic hypothesis is that they are particular and singular in some way." John Grube in the Introduction to this book speaks contemptuously as well of the "regional novel" which tends to be about people who have "some aspirations to cultural identity." Whether or not Watson shares these views (she is applauded in this Introduction for describing her book as an "anti-regional novel") the statements tell us a good deal more about the writer and his neo-colonial culture than about the novel.

The main body of this paper consists of a review of selected literature in three overlapping historical periods: the period of fully developed British imperialism extending roughly to Confederation; the ensuing long period of internal colonialism, which was at its peak before the 1930's; and the period of American imperialism. The last period is discussed in two phases which affect Canadian regions unevenly. One is the process of assimilation; the second, the achievement of this assimilation in the metropolitan areas. Internal colonialism is a corollary of both periods of imperialism, and did not cease with the influx of American-owned industries. On the contrary, it was largely responsible for that development. Nonetheless, there was a period between 1860 and the 1930's during which the internal bourgeoisie were the dominant power in Canada. Between the first and second world wars, this power shifted to American corporate owners, and the internal elite again operated as a satellite rather than a controlling power.

British Imperialism

A colony is a population engaged in the extraction of resources from an undeveloped territory for a mother country. Staples are exported, manufactured goods imported, indigenous industry discouraged, and monetary policies tied to imperial advantages. The colony typically begins as an outpost of empire, that is, a place to which sons of the empire are sent for periods of duty rather than a place of permanent settlement. Indigenous populations (in Canada this included the French as well as Indians and Inuit) are used as a floating resource-extraction work-force or as agricultural workers. Since it does not have permanence and is but a way-station within an army or company (Hudson's Bay) career, the colony has an aura of mystery and adventure; the indigenous peoples are variously savages and romantic antagonists.

Within such a framework one might consider the romantic mythologies about the "Great Canadian North" written in England by English poets; the garrison novel by Frances Brooks, *The History of Emily Montague* (1769), and numerous romantic interpretations of Indians and Indian wars of which *Wacousta* (1832) survives. Those who choose to settle in the colony write for a home market, and particularly for prospective immigrants at home – the essays of Susanna Moodie and her sister Catherine Parr Traill fall into this category with *The Backwoods of Canada* (1836), *Roughing It in the Bush* (1852), and others from the 1830's to 1850's. There is a straightforward character to this kind of literature. The reality of the colony and the official interpretation are congruent; no one pretends that this is other than an outpost of empire. Imperialism is still a "good" word. Those who carry its message do so without hesitation; there is no conflict of interest, no need to judge the merits of the case.

But colonies, if they survive, require settlers. Settlers cannot make an unquestioned virtue of imperial values; cannot imitate with credibility what they have not personally known; develop conflicting loyalties as the needs of their adopted and then native land diverge from those of the empire. Second generations, natives prior to colonization, and immigrants from different cultures (the people imperialists call "ethnic groups") are all in this situation. Settlers with connections to the mother culture have the edge, of course: they can continue to perceive themselves as spokesmen of empire where their countrymen have the monopoly on local technological development, industry, banking and monetary policy, land policies and legislation. Such control ensures that its possessors will determine which aspects of the mother culture will be diffused throughout the colony, and permits the neglect or suppression of alternative cultures. Nonetheless, even the "preferred" settlers are not genuine imperialists, and theirs is a more puzzled literature than that of the temporary frontiersmen.

One finds the beginnings of the puzzlement, the evaluation of imperial virtues, in the sketches of Haliburton's *The Clockmaker....* (1835) and articles by Egerton Ryerson in *The Christian Guardian* in the 1830's and *History of the Loyalists of America* in the 1850's. These remain firmly within British imperial culture, written by Loyalists and their progeny. But they manifest an emerging identification with the colony itself which is missing in earlier literature.

Internal Colonialism

Within the framework of the British fur and timber trade, a settlement of Anglophone merchants, land-speculators, moneylenders, and occasional farmers mushroomed along the St. Lawrence, into the southern valleys of Upper Canada, and throughout the Atlantic regions. The material basis of the settlement continued to be the export-import trade in staples. From the Atlantic, fish and raw (square) timber were exported to Britain, the timber to be cut and turned over to manufacturing there. From the interior the furs continued to arrive, to be handled, priced, perhaps finished, and shipped out of Montreal ports by Montreal merchants. Grain, other agricultural products, minerals, were likewise shipped through the ports of Montreal, and the merchants grew sufficiently wealthy to establish the first banks, insurance and investment houses, and to begin their construction ventures with canals and railroads.

The merchants were one with land speculators, bankers, railroad financiers – and politicians. The Council of Twelve in Halifax, the Family Compact in Upper Canada, the Chateau Clique in Montreal monopolized both commerce and legislative posts in the provinces. But the building of a trans-continental railway required more financial support from the public purse than provincial legislatures could manipulate. The railway became a necessity as fur petered out, and wheat promised higher returns. The solution was confederation, a joining together of speculators and investors who could, in the name of an independent nation, direct tax monies to their private ventures and borrow from abroad for further expansion.

British imperial preference regulations had ensured that neither technology nor machines legally entered the colony, and skilled craftsmen were strongly discouraged from emigrating. These restrictions, together with a banking policy that prohibited direct loans for industrial development, had successfully maintained the colonial dependence on British manufactured goods. The policies were solidly supported by financiers in the colony, whose wealth depended on staples exports and manufacturing imports.

But as the century neared halfway the advantages of maintaining Canada as a colony were lessening in the light of the disadvantages of keeping the United States at arms-length. While Canadian manufacturing was stifled in child-birth, America was becoming a major industrial nation. By mid-century, the impact was already felt in Canada as well as in Britain. The American north-eastern states provided a huge market for square timber, and as soon as imperial preferences were relaxed the export routes shifted southwards. Simultaneously, American firms began buying up timber lands in Ontario and Quebec, establishing sawmills and pulp mills there or shipping their timber raw across the border. American industries were also hungry for capital, and Canadian investors (continuing to restrict loans to indigenous manufacturers) scurried over to the New York Stock Exchange (where by the 1880's the Bank of Montreal was a leading lender). American branch-plants were established in Canada some time before Confederation, and their numbers increased (although not steadily: variations in tariffs and export prices, imperial preference terms and so forth caused fluctuations in the pattern).

By the turn of the century, the relationship between Canada and the United States was established; it was in many (but not all) respects a repetition of the colonial relationship. One of the important differences was the development of industry – American-owned, and still dependent on raw materials extracted in Canada, but industry nonetheless – along the U.S. border in Ontario and Quebec.

This industry created an industrial heartland in Canada, and for a period (the period during which American industries still required Canadian financial backing) consolidated the financial power of an indigenous elite. The Halifax merchants lost their timber trade and control of their resources once Confederation concentrated taxing powers in the Federal government. The western provinces were, from the beginning, resource hinterlands.

Canadian Pacific, the material embodiment of the financiers in the heartland, transported wheat and minerals from the western regions through to the central regions, on to Britain and the States; dealt in land speculation based on the enormous grants attached to the railway charters; and collaborated with the banks in determining interest rates and loan-policies for dependent farmers. The only drawback to all of this, from the point of view of impeccable imitations of British landlords, was the need to populate western farmlands with non-British settlers. As one writer indelicately put it while referring to the 1919 Winnipeg General Strike:

> "As to shipping aliens out of the country, lock stock and barrel, for humane motives this is not possible in the present state of a half-starved Europe. In the aggregate there are a few millions thus to be disposed of, and Canada requires their labour, since British emigration is in the re-arranging state owing to lack of transportation."[2]

This is the economic and social background to literature during that century. Yet one could read the whole of the literature and scarcely know that the Prairies were populated by Ukrainians, Poles, Jews, Hungarians, Rumanians, Ruthenians, Estonians, Finns, Scandinavians, Germans, Dutch, and many others; that a railway was built with what amounted to indentured labour by Chinese, Irish and other immigrants with "non-preferred" status; that the far Western coast contained two-class towns seething with anger and frequently erupting into strikes and warfare; that the farmers knew they were being bilked by the "eastern establishment"; that not only Winnipeg workers but many others failed to share in the wealth of Toronto-based crafts-guild trade unions; that racism was endemic, poverty widespread. The literature, were it read for its "truth" value, would pretty seriously mislead a reader into thinking that the Prairies were populated only by Scotsmen whose endurance, courage, humour and tolerance were altogether remarkable.

There is a widespread notion that Canadian literature prior to the "modern" period (whenever that is) is rich in relevation about regions and ethnic groups. We rather frequently read dismissals of "regional and ethnic idylls" from which we have finally emerged. But where this literature is kept remains a mystery.

There are two models about Icelandic immigrants in the 1920's (Salverson, *The Viking Heart*, 1923, and Ostenso, *Wild Geese*, 1925). There are several novels, romances, and sketches about Scottish and other hinterland British immigrants to rural Ontario, the Prairies, and the Maritimes. Among these one might include *Sky Pilot* (1899) and the several Glengarry books (1900-1910) by Connor; *Trooper and Redskin* (1880's) by North West Mounted Police Lance-Corporal Donkin; *The Story of Louis Riel* (1885) by a Torontonian named Collins whose knowledge of the events and region were happily admitted to be scanty. Add to these Montgomery, *Anne of Green Gables* (1908); Pick, *Next Year* (1928); McClung, *Sowing Seeds in Danny* and others (circa 1920's). These "ethnic" novels were buttressed by the last fond romances in true imperial fashion by de la Roche (*Jalna*, 1927, and subsequent novels), and essays by Leacock (*Sunshine Sketches*, 1912, and others) which, their stock-humour notwithstanding, were firmly embedded in British imperial values.

That is pretty well Canadian fiction through the 1920's. There are three exceptions outside poetry. A passerby, Duncan, wrote *The Imperialist* (1904), and another passerby, Bindles, wrote *The Frontiersman* (1908). Frederick Grove, a transplated European with a flair for self-creation in fiction, wrote four novels about Manitoba and Ontario, all of which marginally caught the regional quality of life while concentrating on family crises. His characters seem more suited to urban Europe than rural Canada, but given the vacuum of Western Canadian literature he stands out as a single and rather lonely contributor (*Settlers of the Marsh*, 1925; *Our Daily Bread*, 1928; *The Yoke of Life*, 1930, and *Fruits of the Earth*, 1933; also essays in *Over Prairie Trails*, 1922).

The puzzle then is surely not why Canadians wrote regional and ethnic idylls. *In fact, they did not write regional or any realistic portrayals of immigrant experience.* One wonders, first, why not, and, second, why do they think they did?

The explanation appears to lie in the fact that Canada remained a colony long after the "declaration of independence" (or the accepting of it, since the removal of imperial preferences provided little choice). This century was a period of consolidation of economic power for a Canadian elite based in Toronto and Montreal; a period of establishing its members first as the purveyors of hinterland resources to imperial Britain, then, capitalizing on the original British base and connections, as the movers of new hinterland resources to the United States. The British origins continued to be important: the elite's protected position depended on keeping the hinterland within Canada, restricting Americans to both a particular region and the manufacturing sector. The banks and utilities remained within Canadian control, agents for consolidation of power vis-a-vis the Canadian hinterland.

The United States, by contrast, was bent on becoming its own imperial power. Eschewing its imperial origins, it set out on the creation of a new race. The "melting pot" concept had sufficient reality to generate a genuine ethnic fiction. The regions, while clearly dominated by the North-East, early developed their own mini-metropoles within which regional literature could emerge. Canada, deliberately staying British and tied to a single metropolitan base, came up with the "mosaic" to explain her reluctance to assimilate "foreigners." Owing to the virtual exclusion of non-British immigrants from the predominant culture, the contrasts, comparisons, mutual awareness and all that serves to bring the balance of involvement and distance were missing. The closest a Canadian could come to ethnic group literature was either unintentional (as in the Scottish mythologies) or imperceptive and genuinely imperial. Connor's deservedly forgotten book, *The Foreigners* (1909) is a manifestation of this. The message here is that non-British immigrants to the Prairies are really quite human after all, as evidenced in the solution to the tale: the foreigner (British people cannot be foreigners any more than they are ethnics) marries an Anglo-angel.

An interesting feature of this internal colonialism is that the proselytizers were predominantly Scots Presbyterians. What they chose to represent as imperial culture was not an aristocratic version. It was a transported colonial version to yet another colony. What saved it from being deadly in its double colonialism was a continuing resentment of English superiority, occasionally manifested in humour. The Scots had no hesitation in being the imperialist evangelical corps with respect to non-British immigrants; there they benefited from the imperial connection. Where they settled into more homogeneous Anglo communities, they were reminded of their inferior status. Their literature reflects the two situations very clearly. It is a continuing sermon on the virtues of British civilization and Christian values as it moves west; and more perplexed and subdued in its imperialist considerations as it moves toward Central Ontario and the Atlantic region.

Combined with the Scots sermons were second-generation hesitations by the sons of Anglicans on the fringe of the elite. Theirs was a particularly poignant situation: they were of the empire, yet constantly reminded that, as colonial subjects, they were second-rate. The problem was nicely stated by Archibald Lampman in a letter to Charles G. D. Roberts in the 1880's:

> Like most young fellows about me, I had been under the depressing conviction that we were situated hopelessly on the outskirts of civilization where no art and literature could be done by any of our companions, still more useless to expect that we could do it ourselves.[3]

These features of a colonial society would explain why a strong regional literature did not emerge in Anglophone Canada. But one would need to go further to explain the widespread notion that such a literature existed. Three possible explanations are suggested. One is that the country was officially labelled a mosaic, and the *myth* continued through to the 1960's that imported cultures were encouraged to express their colourful selves as artistically as they felt able. Since ethnicity and regionalism overlapped, a non-reader aware of the mythology would reasonably assume that "out there," where curious and quaint cultures dotted the Western frontier, there must be an indigenous regional literature. A second explanation would lie with the closeness of American culture, and the importation of its literature. Regional literatures were prominently labelled as such and featured as proud developments in the melting-pot culture of the U.S. A clue to their pervasiveness is given in the Grube Introduction[4] mentioned earlier: the examples of regionalism provided there are American examples.

The third explanation concerns the presence of one alternative culture in Canada that persistently displayed itself and refused to die out or suffer in silence. If it seems curious to think of the Anglo-culture struggling to survive against the French (who was it that was conquered?), it may be because our colonial interpretation of Canadian history has left us with a half-tale of the way it was. Where Americanism could afford to be a hodge-podge guided largely by materialistic instincts, Anglo-Canadianism had constantly to define itself in contradistinction to that monolithic French, ultra-montanist tradition in its midst. The more determined the French culture was in its quest for survival, the more dogmatic, unyielding, and explicit the Anglo-culture became. The notion that somewhere there is a rich regional and ethnic culture is a reflection of an unwilling recognition that Quebec was producing the strongest and most vital art and literature on the continent.

The Process of Assimilation

American industry moved over the border in a steady progression throughout the late nineteenth century, but the influx noticeably increased in volume during the 1920's, and again in the two decades after World War II. Industry itself had undergone a significant change during the first world war: shifting from relatively small and regionally specific manufacturing plants headed by resident owners, to relatively large and regionally dispersed interated complexes headed by non-resident directors and specially trained and mobile managers. The war's end left manufacturers with excess capacity; they filled it by diversifying their products and expanding their territories.

Among the many consequences of this shift in organization was a greatly expanded opportunity ladder in urban centres for clerical, managerial and technically trained workers. The opportunities for skilled workers changed as well, but the changes were more disturbing: the number of marketable new skills increased, but many previously valuable skills became obsolete. In mass production plants, unskilled workers found relatively well-paid jobs provided they could stand the pace, the noise, and the individuation (workers situated side-by-side, each picking up where the previous one left off, but not working interdependently as in a group sense).

Another of the consequences was a greatly expanded demand for raw resources, and an increasing tendency toward integration of control by large manufacturing concerns over both resources and sales outlets, production and distribution. The same corporations were everywhere; the process of consolidation and concentration of industrial wealth speeded up. Because the manufacturing corporations were mainly American in Canada, it was these corporations which – except for Canadian Pacific – became the dominant resource extractors throughout the country.

The effect of American expansion in the industrial heartland was not duplicated in most of the hinterland regions. The labour force that developed in Central Canada could not emerge in the Atlantic, the Prairies, B.C., or the North where industry meant resource extraction rather than manufacturing. The extractive industries employed mainly unskilled and semiskilled workers; others turned to governments for employment. They gave rise to company tours and to haphazard combinations of rural and industrial areas. Throughout these regions the natural landscape which attracted industries suffered wounds. Those who had lived off and with the land were torn between the need for a cash-income and their rural attachments to a natural environment. Alternatives to working in the mills and mines steadily decreased: small sawmills could neither compete nor obtain forestry permits; small farms could not market goods or produce them "efficiently"; land speculators and tourist resorts increased the market value of land for non-farm use and inflated local prices. Work in the big mills and mines provided a steady income for those who could obtain it, but it meant losing both independence and community.

In some areas, particularly in Alberta and B.C., there were certain benefits to the influx of American resource industries. American oil companies, their other effects notwithstanding, provided the first opportunity for local populations to escape British imperialism, and internal colonialism. In the long run this turns out to mean substituting one imperial master for another, but for two generations it has meant release and welcome change. The grandsons of homesteaders who become engineers in the Fort MacMurrays of the North are uneasy mixtures of American technician-consumers and rural isolates, but they are at last definable in terms other than "ethnic."

In B.C., as well, American money has permitted the growth of industries not controlled by "the East." The results are not dissimilar as far as resource extraction is concerned: minerals and timber or pulp are shipped out either way, whether by Canadian Pacific or American mining corporations. The difference is simply in a loosening of the British-styled internal colonial grip.

American culture came along with the industries to the hinterlands as well as to Central Canada. But again, with a difference in reception. The manufacturing region shares the social base of the imported culture: both the consumer goods and the media image are central aspects of standardized urban centres. But elsewhere the contrasts between image and reality are recognizable. American culture as portrayed in the media and taught in the branch-plant universities is more noticeably foreign where there is no manufacturing base, where there is not a complete class structure, where unemployment is a chronic feature of existence.

The literatures of the different regions reflect these fundamental differences in economy and society. Most novels of the period are attempts to portray "reality" and the reader is invited to approach literature as "truth." The predominant style is literal rendering, straight-forward story-telling, sparing use of symbols and fairly simple metaphors.

As truth, some of the literature does provide signposts for a foreigner. One does begin to hear about the harsher aspects of Canadian society. Baird's *Waste Heritage* (1939) is no doubt a literary flop, but it is one of a kind in its attempt to deal with the garrisoned and rioting unemployed in the Vancouver of the

1930's. Sinclair Ross's stark portrait of prairie towns in the 1930's has similar truth value in *As For Me and My House* (1941). Garner's *Cabbagetown* (1968) is one of the rare glimpses of depression slums in urban centres. Very occasional portraits of ethnic and immigrant groups from the inside have provided insights, such as Wiebe's study of the Mennonites in Saskatchewan, *Peace Shall Destroy Many* (1962), and Wiseman's delineation of Jewish immigrants to Winnipeg, *The Sacrifice* (1956).

Through several novels by women about women, one learns a good deal about specific regions, male-female relationships, families, occupational cultures, and social change as well as women and men. (For example: Wilson's *Hetty Dorval* (1947) and *Swamp Angel* (1962); and Laurence's *The Stone Angel* (1964) and *A Jest of God* (1966) and *The Fire Dwellers* (1969).

Nonetheless, it is not the truth value that makes this literature sociologically interesting. It is rather the gathering together of assumptions and arguments which provide an overall description of emerging values within Canada; and the contrasts between these descriptions for different regions of the country.

I have not undertaken a systematic content analysis of novels and poetry between about 1930 and the present time, and would not want to play an Atwood-style reduction of all themes to that which coincides with my own predilections; yet tentatively I find in the literature a persistent distrust of technological development, an equally persistent self-righteousness about rural virtues. This doesn't come across as a victim mentality so much as an intense concern with remaining (or returning to) a state of purity and wholeness. Moral – which is to say, social – issues take precedence over private agonies: the latter act primarily to demonstrate the former rather than parade as the central problems.

These social concerns are to pervasive that novels tend to be vehicles for their expression, characters puppets for their display. The moral concerns which inform the work of Callaghan and MacLennan in the 1930's, 1940's, early 1950's (as in *They Shall Inherit the Earth*, 1935; *Such is My Beloved*, 1934; *Barometer Rising*, 1941; and *Two Solitudes*, 1945), have their parallels in American literature of the period, but in Canada such concerns monopolised literature. There is no parallel for

Hemingway's narcissistic concerns. Scott Fitzgerald's premonition that Freud would become an American phenomenon served him well, but Freud was as alien to Canada in the early 1950's as to occupied Vienna.

In the more rural hinterlands of Canada psychological portraits were even more subjected to social concerns. It was not wealth as such which defined the devil, it was industry, technology, crowds without community. From Grove's early statement about the mill which seemed: "... as if no human could stop it; as if, even though the whole population of the earth perished, it would go on producing flour till it had smothered the globe." (*Master of the Mill*), one proceeds through one expression after another of the same fear. Protagonists find peace and salvation by turning their backs on urban societies, though their private experiences of it may differ considerably. Ethel Wilson's Maggie finds her solution in a remote B.C. fishing lodge in *Swamp Angel* (1954); Raddall's Isabel finds it in the isolation of Sable Island and a blind lover in *The Nymph and the Lamp* (1950); Buckler's David seeks it in the farm home of a Nova Scotia childhood in *The Mountain and the Valley* (1952); Evans' returned soldier rejects Vancouver for Northern homesteading, and his Pitt family recognizes that its Indian reserve contains virtues unknown in Prince Rupert in *The New Front Line* (1927) and *Mist on the River* (1954).

These were written in a period of rural to urban migration throughout North America. American literature was meanwhile concentrating on the same move, but taking the opposite view. Yet there is no particular mystery as to why Canadian literature took this turn. These hinterlands are rural: urban society, industrial society, encroaches, it does not slowly emerge. It is abruptly there, belonging to someone else far away; it is just as abruptly gone. When the mine dries up or the timber loses its market, the foreign owners remove the source of employment on which a population, meanwhile, has come to depend; and, in fact, has no choice but to depend. The writers perceive, and represent the insecurity, the lack of control over local events, the unpredictable ways of foreign technology. People become anonymous in the imposed society, lose themselves working the imposed technology. Personal identity is therefore a social, not a psychological, problem.

> Awful, revolting daydream of a way of life. Appalling love that keeps us clinging to this rope. Bullying, bloody mine that has no use for pleasurable, timid times, and I'll be dead before I know them. I swear that at times I'd have done myself kindness by walking the road of the two dollar whore, please God forgive me, but at least in shocking, gaudy tinsel and stuff, I'd have known who I was. For who and what am I here? Anonymous in an anonymous speck, where even those with the strength to save themselves would walk their legs off trying to find the exit to this crippling town, their eyes and hearts and brains are so packed with dust. – Pinsent, *John and the Missus* (1974)

This seems to me to contrast rather starkly with much of American post-war literature, and with some of the current metropolitan literature now being published in Canada. In the metropolitan centres one discovers a literature obsessed with entirely private dilemmas. Psychology rather than sociology is the interest of authors; pathology rather than morality the guiding theme.

There is nothing in Canadian literature up to the 1960's, and still nothing in the hinterland literature, comparable with, for one example, the American picaresque travelogues of a Nabokov through those of a Miller and a Pirsig. The endless ride across a continent in an embarrassingly public search for private identity and personal values is a peculiarly American fiction. It is also a peculiarly American reality. The homogeneous society with its similar gadgetry, symbols, signs and values is represented in mile after mile of road, night after night of motels, day after day of cafes. Everyone is on the move, everyone is interchangeable. It is not moral issues or windmills which impel the search: it is, rather, a sense of being anyone and selfless or belonging nowhere in particular. The theme is picked up in the mid-1960's in Montreal by Leonard Cohen in *Beautiful Losers* (1966), but there is no counterpart elsewhere in Canada.

Poets at the centre who style themselves spokesmen of the working class may characterize – or caricature, perhaps – the unionized working class of the manufacturing regions. Layton's representation of what he perceives as working-class vulgarity grows, I would guess, on a vivid portrayal of the contrasting bourgeoisie. It may be the lack of a thriving bourgeoisie as much as a different kind of working class in genuine frontier communities which makes his poetry so regionally specific as to be out-of-place in them. People in northern Canada, most of B.C., much of the Prairies and the Atlantic regions tend to talk about the seasons, natural features of the landscape, genuine problems of survival; and they tend to be puritanical in the sense of recognizing the legitimacy of certain moral (and verbal) codes for the protection of their neighbours. They are individualistic but their interpretation of individualism is not that of the poets who romanticize personal freedom: they tend rather to emphasize personal strength, personal responsibility, resourcefulness and reliability. They are tied in to communities, and treat these ties without sentimentality: survivial depends on interdependence.

A densely populated urban society dependent on manufacturing and financial industries is a region in which the natural physical environment and the seasons become relatively unimportant to "making a living." Seasons are external events, worthy of passing comment only. Natural environments become places to go while on holiday. Much of what is tolerable in life becomes what one can purchase on high incomes. Over the span of three generations in this environment, the skills associated with economies in which seasons and natural settings are crucial elements are lost. Urban populations in general do not have survival techniques independent of manufacturing industries. Neither do they have the perceptions customary to rural populations: they cannot see or hear acutely in non-urban environments. There is no reason to suppose that their writers, emerging in such environments, are exceptions to the rule.

By contrast, the accompanying theme of rural hinterland fiction is intense involvement with nature. No doubt the great expanses, exuberant rain-forests, extraordinary mountains, appalling, powerful sea have their independent effects on a people. But the same topographical features elsewhere, including the United States, do not elicit as overwhelming – or overwhelmed – a response. I don't see the response in terms of victimization, however; it is rather part of the identification of self in hinterland regions. Nature is one with a rural and (the vagaries of crops notwithstanding) predictable life. It is one with communities but not with crowds; one with isolation but not loneliness. Nature as perceived by a hinterland people caught in a resource-extraction economy is the antithesis of industrialism.

This may be linked with the current interest in Indian culture, although the more pressing explanation must lie in Indian land claims. These pose an immediate threat on two fronts: to those who would continue exploiting resources in a fashion which commits cultural genocide against Indians; and to those who base their moral integrity on the unimpeachability of legal protection for private property. If aboriginal land claims are respected (which, given the legal precedents, they should be) the relative positions of Indians and whites would abruptly change, and jobs dependent on the status quo would be threatened; if the land claims are rejected (as, given the context and history of treatment of Indians, they probably will be), the status of legal principles with respect to property is thrown in doubt. This represents a moral as well as economic challenge to Anglo-society, and it elicits many of the same sympathetic liberal responses from authors (e.g., Evans, *Mist on the River* [1954]; Ryga, *Ecstasy of Rita Joe* [1964]) as the French-Anglo conflict in Montreal elicited at an earlier stage before the battlelines were clearly drawn (e.g., MacLennan, *Two Solitudes* [1945]; Graham, *Earth and High Heaven* [1944]).

The Achievement of Assimilation

The characteristic which most quickly identifies any dominant group is its tendency to assume that its welfare is everybody's welfare, its will the general will, and its values everybody's values. Men assume this of women, whites of Indians, Anglophones of Francophones, Americans of Canadians, and Torontonians of the rest of Canada.

Donald Stephens in an assessment of the short story in Canada of the 1960's represents the view:

> "There is then a gradual shift from the rural to the urban, but this shift is more marked in the sensibility revealed than

it is in the setting employed. The writers are obviously more sophisticated in their view of human nature. . . ."[5]

It is not difficult to appreciate the enormous gulf in sensitivity between Ralph Connor and Margaret Laurence, or Mazo de la Roche and Ethel Wilson, but the gulf is not appropriately described as a shift from rural to urban or backwoods to modern. I make a quibble about a word because I think two serious problems arise as a consequence of its inappropriate use. One is that writers outside Toronto and Montreal, and especially those who choose to live in and write about the non-urban societies which make up most of Canada, are unnecessarily handicapped by the geocentric urbanites' version of Canada. The other is that such phrases treat genuine urban writers – Leonard Cohen, Iriving Layton, Robertson Davies, Hugh Garner, Margaret Atwood and Mordecai Richler, for example – as if they were not as regionally based as all others.

To continue with Mr. Stephens:

> The mosaic which marks so obviously the Canadian heritage has also made it easier for Canadians to work with the contemporary problems of alienation, compassion, and love, which makes up so much a part of the themes of contemporary fiction. . . .[6]

There is more than a problem of geocentrism in an identification of compassion and love as particularly contemporary problems, but we'll try to ignore that and concentrate on what Mr. Stephens seems to have been getting at. It is probably true that if one were obliged to choose a few descriptive terms for much of contemporary art, one would choose what contemporary critics define as modern: the mystic and often mythic search for private salvation; the quest for roots and community combined with an intense and tortured individualism; the alienation of human souls caged not only in a world of strangers but in a world of alien machines, symbols, cement structures. What could be more particularistic than this: it describes the dilemmas of an urban people in an urban, capitalist, industrial society of the post-1950's.

Of course, an increasing proportion of the Canadian population and of the world's population lives in these urban societies. There are common characteristics that cross national borders. Bureaucracy, the modes of industrial production, the nature of work in industrial settings, housing, population density, shopping patterns, family life, modes of transportation and communication: all tend toward a standardized pattern in urban situations. Konrad's *The Case Worker* (1974) is only in part specific to Budapest and a state-capitalist system: much of the social worker's existence is familiar to Canadian counterparts. These common threads don't make the literature more universal, modern, cosmopolitan, or sophisticated: they make it more accessible to a larger reading public, which is not the same thing.

Both content and style of literature are affected by economic underpinnings. Tracing Canadian (and other) literatures through the past couple of centuries, literary historians are sometimes satisfied to identify progress in a shift from mythology through romanticism to realism and on to symbolism. A chronological listing of literature does suggest such a developmental process – although there are distinct regional deviations – but all of the attributes of genuine universality are aspects of any of the stages or none of them. If university is taken to mean the capacity to make comprehensible to outsiders a familiar culture, that is, not eliminating regional roots but revealing them; if it is taken to mean a capacity to appreciate simultaneously the intensity of the culture and the foreigness of it to non-members, that is, to maintain distance even while being intensely involved; if it has these characteristics, then any of the styles is capable of bearing a universalistic literature.

If that is the case, then changes in styles are not changes toward some greater perfection, not progress in any artistic sense, but rather reflections of changes in the culture which creates the artists and provides an audience for them. A literature which poses the problem of personal identity as the ultimate puzzle is one which directs the reader's attention away from the social roots of identity; one which fragments reality has a similar function. Without attempting to impose a one-to-one relationship between society and literary representation, one might reasonably expect that both content and style derive from certain "realities" in the society such as – in the cases suggested – an atomizing, individuating process linked with styles of work and material exigencies, and complex technologies which prohibit full views of whole entities. Symbolic representations rather literally represent a symbolizing culture and a chaotic, artificial lifestyle. They are "realistic" portrayals of metropolitan societies. (One should add quickly, in anticipation of the complaint from one such as wrote the introduction to Watson's book, that a metropolite imposes a metropolitan interpretation on other and unlike cultures; a reader understands the relationship between hinterland and metropolis in such versions, and the metropolitan experience of the writer, but not the internal cohesion of the hinterland culture.)

The urban society in Canada has many of the characteristics of American metropolitan centres. Physically, it contains the inadequate housing, squalid streets, division between living and working quarters, suburbs cut off from the centre or vice-versa, the steady elimination of natural environment. Socially, it contains crowds and individuals rather than communities; a highly stratified labour force maintained in dividend condition by an unequal distribution of wealth and the largely ideological assignment of difference to vague notions of functional importance; pockets of wealth, pockets of poverty; racism and class conflict.

Ideologically there are differences between the satellite cities and their American parents. The British cradle left its mark, the nearness of the resource hinterland both in space and memory prohibits complete absorption, and the knowledge of foreign ownership cannot be eliminated where its signs and consequences are so pervasive. Nonetheless, the assimilation of American values is well advanced: the emphasis on mobility, change, personal success, individual freedom – all attributes of a well-disciplined labour force within a "private enterprise" economy; the connecting of success with wealth and corporate position; the obliteration of distinctiveness; the ridicule of puritanical moral codes suitable only to genuine communities. There is less room than there was during the 1930's and 1940's for moderate statements of opposition, for varying positions. One accepts or wholly rejects; the monolithic quality of metropolitan culture leaves little choice to the rebel but revolution.

Literature of urban Canada reflects the dilemmas, and is well read not as Canadian literature, of which it is only a small part, but as the literature of a satellite manufacturing economy. Giant city-wide tomato juice taste-tests, unwed office stenos, cocktail parties in flats, meetings in laundromats, store-bought hobbies, legal careers and definitive editions suitable for theses: these are the props identified by Atwood in *The Edible Woman* (1970). The people in Marian McAlpine's social world have no skills beyond filling out forms and snarling up bed-sheets. One is reminded occasionally that there is another world out there, but it is behind us. It shows up in such things as a sentimental calendar sent by a third cousin who runs a service station "back home." True to form, the calendar becomes a calculating tool for roommate Ainsley's planned parenthood. *Surfacing* (1972) is an angry repetition of similar themes. There are the make-believe friends, the make-believe lovers who all "disowned their parents long ago, the way you are supposed to," and a home ground prominently labelled "foreign territory." The lack of skills for the creation of a non-American lifestyle are rather heavily drawn.

Beautiful Losers, however, is not a protest. Whether it is a search for sainthood (as Pacey argues)[7] or the ultimate orgasm, which probably amount to the same thing, indexed and blanketed by an overwhelming dose of McLuhanesque myths and goddesses, it comes across as the ultimate acquiescence. The global village becomes a moving car, usually one in which the passengers are preoccupied with manipulating their natural equipment in time to the flashings of passing neon signs. Disengagement means losing oneself, as in biblical terms, in order to find oneself: but to find oneself a universal thing, a non-person, a one without particular emotions. Cut off from society, cut off from nature, cut off from oneself, disembodied. This is the ultimate in man as technician – said the radio as it turned itself on.

Yet the alternative is escape and yet more imitation or romance. Robertson Davies tried the deliberately regional novel with such condescension that as parody it was unintentionally humorous (*Leaven of Malice, Mixture of Frailities*, 1951–1958). Then, with Fowles and Hesse leading the way to yet a new "universal" literature and mythology, he attempted to combine the Presbyterian roots with mysticism (*Fifth Business*, 1970;

The Manticore, 1972). Here, Davies observed that the Canadian North quite naturally gave rise to mystery and mysticism; again, this is perhaps true but primarily for the urban dweller rather than the person living in the north.

The more engaging urban literature is deliberately regional. Mordecai Richler (*Duddy Kravitz*, 1959) is successful because he is fully occupied with St. Urbain Street. There is no pretence here that St. Urbain Street is like Yonge or Hastings, that Duddy's heritage symbolizes all immigrants, that his amoral land-deals represent some great dilemma. Nor is he an imitation of Schulberg's *Sammy*: the two operate in quite different cultures. I'm aware that Richler is in disrepute for his exploitation of the marginal Canadian role; I find *Duddy* nonetheless more convincing Canadian literature than Atwood's too-much protesting.

One of the ironies of Canadian society and literature becomes apparent in reading urban literature of the late 1960's and early 1970's. The Canadian "mosaic" was supposed to define the Canadian Prairies; to legitimate a modest apartheid. While it is still the Prairies which have the largest proportion of non-French, non-British descendents, it is the metropolitan cities which provide a context for ethnic conflict and specifically ethnic literature. Examples are Clarke's illumination of prejudice and conflict for West Indians in Toronto (*The Meeting Point*, 1967; *When He Was Young...*, 1971); Moore's characterization of Irish immigrants in Montreal (*The Luck of Ginger Coffey*, 1960); and the considerable volume of both Anglo-novels and translations of French novels about Montreal (e.g., MacLennan, *Return of the Sphinx*, 1967; Aquin, *Prochain Episode*, tr. 1967; Gélinas' Play, *Yesterday the Children were Dancing*, tr. 1967; Desbiens, *The Impertinences of Frère Un Tel*, tr. 1965). It is the contrast that gives rise to perceptions and the need to explain; but it is, as well, the genuine conflict and violence that erupts in these cities and which, given an ideology now of equality, cannot be justifiably ignored. Here is one of the many contradictions within liberal capitalism. It both creates many of the conditions for racism and violence, and provides the ideological context for exposure and condemnation.

Writers as Representatives

Torontonians of the radical variety share with others of non-radical persuasion a tendency to view the rest of Canada as their own hinterland. Consequently, they take for granted that the assimilation of Toronto is the assimilation of Canada.

One could hardly pretend that any part of Canada is unaffected by American culture, but the history to date suggests that the effects are not uniform. For all their similarities, Toronto is not Chicago; no more is Halifax, Hamilton or Vancouver, London or Ontario. There are distinctive features to all of these cities, and even more distinctive features to such regions as the fishing villages of Newfoundland, the cariboo ranches in B.C., and the farmlands of the Peace River. The question is not whether all will be assimilated into the continental plastic society – unless all became equally involved in a manufacturing economy that could not happen – but whether each will be able to recognize its separateness and continue to express it in cultural forms as literature.

The potentiality for this expression depends on opportunities for publication and marketing of regional work, and on opportunities for sufficient leisure to write. The first of these is by no means guaranteed in Canada, where publishers and distributors are overwhelmingly American subsidiaries. Low population density adds to the non-marketability, and therefore to the non-publication of books.

However, disadvantages occasionally lead to curious situations. One such is that historical barriers to women in so many other fields (e.g., law, science, management, medicine, academia, mass media) have caused women to turn their artistic and intellectual talents to the writing of literature. Had this been a review of Canadian literature in terms of sex rather than regions, the first and most obvious point would have been the high proportion of women writers during *all* periods of Canadian history. This is the rare area in which men are disadvantaged by the (sometimes written) law that they shall rule the earth. Ruling is a time-consuming business, and, even more serious as an obstacle to writing, it is a mind-consuming pastime.

This curious reversal seems to run contrary to the general observation set out earlier, that literature is largely a product of elites. Women writers are not an elite, but those who have written in Canada have been, by and large, well-educated people whose other daily tasks are incongruous with early training and intellectual capacities. Ethel Wilson and Margaret Laurence are examples of the group: both were submerged at one stage of their lives in child-rearing and husband-tending within their husbands' professional class milieus. It remains the case that most Canadian writers in English, men and women, are descended from (or are themselves) either British or American ancestors, most are from relatively affluent home environments, and most have extended educational histories which occurred in urban environments. Regional literature as a consequence is still mainly a version of regional society as seen by urban women and men of the Anglo middle class, and must reflect their values and concerns.

Summary

I have started with the assumption that literature, all literature, is regional in its representation of society. I have treated universality as a quality of perceptiveness and conveyance of ideas rather than as a social condition. It is my contention that universality may be characteristic of any style and any content – and is therefore not restricted to highly stylized urban literature. In terms of my own (hinterland but hopelessly urban and middle-class) aesthetic tastes, not much Canadian literature is universalistic. I find some of it moralistic to the point of boredom; I find some of the dilemmas portrayed imitative and lacking in depth. However, this is equally true of American, British, other European and translated Third-World literature. There are, after all, very few giants anywhere at any time. Between the two extremes there is a substantial literature which is interesting and informative about this society, whether by intent or by accident. I have argued throughout the paper that this literature may be read as sociological documentation; that it displays in its assumptions, style, content, and concerns, the shifts in Canadian society from a British colony to a British satellite dominated by an internal financial elite, and from this to an American satellite with variations in degree of assimilation into the American continental society.

Notes

1. Desmond Pacey, "The Novel in Canada" (originally in *Queen's Quarterly*, Autumn, 1945), *Essays in Canadian Criticism* (Toronto: Ryerson Press, 1969), p. 28.

2. Colonel J. Hanna McCormick on the "Barr Colony" in Lloydminster, as quoted in Edward McCourt, *The Canadian West in Fiction*, (Toronto: Ryerson, 1970). p. 73.

3. Letter quoted in Clara Thomas, *Our Nature – Our Voices*. Vol. 1 (Toronto: New Press, 1972), p. 46.

4. Grube Introduction in Sheila Watson's *The Double Hook* (1959).

5. Donald Stephens, "The Short Story in English," in *The Sixties, Canadian Writers and Writing of the Decade*, edited by George Woodcock (Vancouver: University of British Columbia, 1969), p. 129.

6. *Loc. cit.*

7. *Op. Cit.*, "The Phenomenon of Leonard Cohen" (1969), pp. 241-265.

APPENDIX

Selected Readings on the Sociology of Literature

Barbu, Z. "Sociological Perspectives in Art and Literature," in Creedy, J. *The Social Context of Art*. London: Tavistock, 1970.

Barnett, J. H. "The Sociology of Art," in Merton, Broom, and Cotterell eds., *Sociology Today*. New York: Basic Books, 1958.

Benjamin, W. *Illuminations: Essays and Reflections*. London: Jonathan Cope, 1970.

Coser, L. *Sociology Through Literature*. Englewood Cliffs: Prentice Hall, 1963.

Escarpit, R. *The Book Revolution*. London: Harrap, 1966.

Fisher, E. *Art Against Ideology*. London: The Penguin Press, 1969.

——, *The Necessity of Art*. London: Penguin Books, 1963.

Goldmann, L. "Criticism and Dogmatism in Literature," in D. Cooper ed., *The Dialectics of Liberation*. London: Pegnuin Books, 1968.

Hoggart, R. "Literature and Society," in MacKenzie ed., *A Guide to The Social Sciences*. London: Weidenfeld and Nicolson, 1966.

Lowenthal, L. *Literature and The Image of Man*. Boston: Beacon Press, 1957.

Lukacs, G. *Solzhenitsyn*. London: Merlin Press, 1971.

Margolies, D. N. *The Function of Literature*. New York: International Publishers, 1969.

Wellek R. and Warren, A. *Literature and Society*. 4th ed. London: Peregrine Books, 1963.

Selected Readings on the Sociology of Art and Literature

Baxandall, L. Ed. *Radical Perspectives in The Arts*, London: Penguin Books, 1972.

Bergin, E. B. "Marxism Psychoanalysis, and Artistic Creativity." *Studies on The Left*. Vol. 1, no. 4, 1961, pp. 114-19.

Field, R. D. "Art and Socialism," *Monthly Review* Vol. 1, no. 1, January 1950, pp. 266-71.

Marx, K. and Engels, F. *On Literature and Art*. New York: International Publishers, 1947.

Matthiessen, F. O. "Marxism and Literature," *Monthly Review* Vol. 4, no. 11, March 1953, pp. 398-400.

Plekhanov, G. *Art and Social Life* (1912). London: Lawrence and Wishart, 1953.

For a bibliography of Canadian literature and Canadian literary critique, see: Gnarowski, M. *A Concise Bibliography of English-Canadian Literature*. Toronto: McClelland and Stewart, 1973, revised edition 1978.

Contributors

Paul Cappon is a social scientist with special interest in the Sociology of Literature and in Canadian and Quebec society. He has taught in the Department of Anthropology and Sociology at the University of British Columbia. He is also author of *Conflits entre Néo-Canadiens et Francophones à Montréal*, Presses de l'Université Laval, Québec, 1974.

James Steele is Professor of English at Carleton University in Ottawa. His special field is Canadian Literature.

Robin Endres is a student of Canadian Literature who is based in Toronto and has taught in the English Departments of various institutions.

Robin Mathews is Professor of English at Carleton University. He is also a noted Canadian poet and, with James Steele, was in the vanguard of the 1960's struggle against the Americanization of Canadian universities.

John Fraser is Associate Professor of Political Science at the University of Waterloo. He has a special interest in European perspectives on Canadian problems.

Patricia Marchak is Associate Professor of Anthropology and Sociology at the University of British Columbia. Patricia Marchak has a special interest in the metropolis-hinterland relationship within Canada.